Published by   Church House Publishing
                Church House
                Great Smith Street
                London SW1P 3NZ

Copyright ©   *The Archbishops' Council 2006*

               First published 2006

    ISBN-13   978-0-7151-2122-1
    ISBN-10   0 7151 2122 7

Printed in England by the University Printing Press, Cambridge

Typeset in Gill Sans and Joanna
Designed by John Morgan studio

Time to Pray

Prayer During the Day and Night Prayer

from Common Worship: Daily Prayer

Church House Publishing

Contents

Introduction

Time to Pray is a pattern of prayer, praise and daily Bible reading that is simple, fresh and accessible. It enables us to create and establish a regular routine of time with God – whatever our lifestyle. While being straightforward and flexible to use, it draws us into a tradition that has been practised by Christians throughout the centuries and continues to be shared across the world today.

Time to Pray creates a framework for praying the Bible. In addition to the space provided for study or reflection on God's word, many of the words and phrases that are used come directly from Scripture. A church in which people pray the Bible together becomes a church which is equipped for proclamation and service.

Using *Time to Pray*: different patterns

Many people have evolved a daily Quiet Time, for reading Scripture and for praying. With this in mind, Prayer During the Day is offered as a framework for personal devotion that can be used at any time of day.

You can use Prayer During the Day as your sole act of prayer and praise, or you can use both Prayer During the Day and Night Prayer in a simple pattern of prayer at the beginning and end of the day.

Prayer During the Day and Night Prayer also work well with small groups and larger congregations, in a variety of contexts.

Time to Pray is a simple starting point for regular daily prayer. Both Prayer During the Day and Night Prayer are part of a larger and more extensive scheme of regular devotion, appropriately entitled *Common Worship: Daily Prayer*. *Daily Prayer* contains the more substantial Morning and Evening Prayer, all the Psalms and a sizeable range of prayers, intercessions and scriptural songs.

Prayer During the Day

Introduction

A pattern for Prayer During the Day is provided for each day of the week. This may be used on that day of the week at any time of year. In addition there is a form of Prayer During the Day for each of the seasons of the Christian year. This may be used throughout the season or at certain high points: for example, the Easter form may be used between Easter and Pentecost, or for the first week of Eastertide, or on Easter Day only.

Setting the scene

Creating a prayerful environment is important for those who are praying by themselves as much as for those who are praying with others. You may find it helpful to establish a special place in which to pray. You might also place an open Bible, a cross, a candle, an icon or another picture in front of you, to give the time and space special significance. You will be able to think of other symbols and simple actions that you can build into your prayer time.

The shape of Prayer During the Day

Prayer During the Day has a simple structure that will quickly develop into a familiar rhythm when used regularly.

Preparation

The opening responses – verses from Scripture – conventionally lead into prayer. You may wish to meditate on the words or still yourself with some music, as you invite the Holy Spirit to inspire you.

If you wish to make a confession to God, this is a good place to do so. If you need some words, there is a confession at the beginning of Night Prayer (page 77).

Praise

At this point you may wish to use your own words to praise God, or to sing a hymn or song. The texts printed in Prayer During the Day introduce us to a selection of well-established traditional and biblical songs of praise, called 'canticles'. (A canticle is a song, most often taken directly from the Bible.)

The Word of God

A psalm and one or more Bible readings are read.

Psalms: Each pattern of Prayer During the Day suggests a psalm or part of a psalm which may be used. These can be found on pages 89–104.

On each day and in each season a more varied pattern of psalms is also suggested. (In order to keep the book to a reasonable length, these psalms have not been printed out.) An even more comprehensive way of reading the psalms can be found in the annual *Common Worship Lectionary* booklet.

There is some advice about how to use the psalms on pages 87–88.

Readings: One of the best ways of hearing God speaking through holy Scripture is to follow a well-constructed pattern of readings day by day. The reading in Prayer During the Day can be

♦ the day's passage from a book of Bible-reading notes.

♦ one or two of the readings for the day in the annual *Common Worship Lectionary* booklet. This provides an Old Testament reading and a New Testament reading each for Morning and Evening Prayer. Choosing one of those tracks to read during your prayer time would give you a path to follow that covers most of the Bible in due course and also echoes the seasons of the Church's year.

♦ the short reading printed in the text of Prayer During the Day. These work well on occasion, but are not intended to provide a balanced biblical diet over a sustained period of time.

Response

The printed text is a minimal, biblical response. You may wish to stay in silence for a while, spend time on personal Bible study, discuss the readings with others (if you are in a group) or sing in praise and worship. The readings may also have stirred you to pray or make confession, in which case you will move on to the next section.

Prayers

This is an opportunity to pray in whatever way comes naturally to you. For each day and season, a suggested list of topics for intercession is offered which you can add to your own requests and thanksgivings. A prayer of confession may also be used.

Drawing prayers together with a collect and the Lord's Prayer is a well-established pattern. (A 'collect' is a 'gathering prayer' – it collects or 'gathers up' the concerns expressed in the prayers.) The collects in Prayer During the Day are all well-loved classic prayers.

The Conclusion

Just as the beginning of Prayer During the Day was indicated by an opening response, so it is brought to an end by a closing prayer. Other endings can be used instead, such as the Grace:

> **The grace of our Lord Jesus Christ,**
> **and the love of God,**
> **and the fellowship of the Holy Spirit,**
> **be with us all evermore.**
> **Amen.**

or the Peace:

> The peace of the Lord be always with you
> *All* **and also with you.**

> *These words may be added*

> Let us offer one another a sign of peace,
> God's seal on our prayers.

Speech, song and silence – some guidance

♦ Singing, however simply, and even on your own, may help you to engage in the worship.

♦ Speaking the responses and prayers and reading the Bible aloud can help you to concentrate and to encounter God. A gentle and regular pace will also help to achieve this.

♦ Silence is an essential element of prayer, reflection and listening to God. Don't forget to make space for this.

♦ Body posture is important, too. Even if you are praying alone you will find that appropriate variation of position makes a positive difference.

Prayer During the Day

Structure

¶ **Preparation**
Opening responses, or another introduction. A Form of Penitence may be used here or in the Prayers.

¶ **Praise**
Either the printed text or another acclamation, hymn or song

¶ **The Word of God**
A psalm, and one or more Bible readings

¶ **Response**
The printed text, or a less formal response

¶ **Prayers**
Intercessions, a Collect and the Lord's Prayer

¶ **The Conclusion**
A closing prayer, dismissal, blessing, or other ending

¶ *Prayer During the Day on Sunday*

Preparation

O God, make speed to save us.

All **O Lord, make haste to help us.**

My heart tells of your word, 'Seek my face.'

All **Your face, Lord, will I seek.**   *Psalm 27.10*

Praise

A hymn, song, canticle, extempore praise or

We praise you, O God,
we acclaim you as the Lord;
all creation worships you,
the Father everlasting.
To you all angels, all the powers of heaven,
the cherubim and seraphim, sing in endless praise:
Holy, holy, holy Lord, God of power and might,
heaven and earth are full of your glory.

from Te Deum Laudamus

The Word of God

Psalm

On any Sunday   Psalm 19 (pages 91–92)

(or)

| *Week 1* | Psalm 20 | *Week 3* | Psalm 115.1-13 |
| *Week 2* | Psalm 34 | *Week 4* | Psalm 116 |

Each psalm or group of psalms may end with

All   **Glory to the Father and to the Son**
and to the Holy Spirit;
as it was in the beginning is now
and shall be for ever. Amen.

Short readings

Week One

In the beginning when God created the heavens and the earth,
the earth was a formless void and darkness covered the face of
the deep, while a wind from God swept over the face of the waters.
Then God said, 'Let there be light'; and there was light. And God
saw that the light was good; and God separated the light from the
darkness. God called the light Day, and the darkness he called Night.
And there was evening and there was morning, the first day.

Genesis 1.1-5

Week Two

If anyone is in Christ, there is a new creation: everything old has
passed away; see, everything has become new! All this is from God,
who reconciled us to himself through Christ, and has given us the
ministry of reconciliation; that is, in Christ God was reconciling the
world to himself.   *2 Corinthians 5.17-19a*

Week Three

The man went away and told the Jews that it was Jesus who had made him well. Therefore the Jews started persecuting Jesus, because he was doing such things on the sabbath. But Jesus answered them, 'My Father is still working, and I also am working.' For this reason the Jews were seeking all the more to kill him, because he was not only breaking the sabbath, but was also calling God his own Father, thereby making himself equal to God.

John 5.15-18

Week Four

I, John, saw a new heaven and a new earth; for the first heaven and the first earth had passed away, and the sea was no more. And I saw the holy city, the new Jerusalem, coming down out of heaven from God, prepared as a bride adorned for her husband. And I heard a loud voice from the throne saying, 'See, the home of God is among mortals. He will dwell with them; they will be his peoples, and God himself will be with them; he will wipe every tear from their eyes. Death will be no more; mourning and crying and pain will be no more, for the first things have passed away.'   *Revelation 21.1-4*

Or, on any Sunday

Wisdom says, 'I was beside him, like a master worker; and I was daily his delight, rejoicing before him always, rejoicing in his inhabited world and delighting in the human race.'   *Proverbs 8.30,31*

Response

Silence, study, song, or words from Scripture, such as

Jesus said, I am the living bread that came down from heaven.

All **Whoever eats of this bread will live for ever.**   *John 6.51a*

Prayers

Prayers may include these concerns:

¶   *The universal Church*
¶   *Bishops, synods and all who lead the Church*
¶   *The leaders of the nations*
¶   *The natural world and the resources of the earth*
¶   *All who are in any kind of need*

The Collect of the day or the following prayer is said

Christ be with me, Christ within me,
Christ behind me, Christ before me,
Christ beside me, Christ to win me,
Christ to comfort and restore me.
Christ beneath me, Christ above me,
Christ in quiet, Christ in danger,
Christ in hearts of all that love me,
Christ in mouth of friend and stranger.

All   **Amen.**   *from St Patrick's Breastplate*

The Lord's Prayer is said (inside back cover).

The Conclusion

May God who made both heaven and earth bless us.

All   **Amen.**

¶ *Prayer During the Day on Monday*

Preparation

O God, make speed to save us.

All **O Lord, make haste to help us.**

Let the words of my mouth and the meditation of my heart

All **be acceptable in your sight, O Lord,
my strength and my redeemer.** *Psalm 19.14*

Praise

A hymn, song, canticle, extempore praise or

I bind unto myself today
the strong name of the Trinity,
by invocation of the same,
the Three in One, and One in Three.
Of whom all nature hath creation;
eternal Father, Spirit, Word:
Praise to the Lord of my salvation,
salvation is of Christ the Lord. *from St Patrick's Breastplate*

The Word of God

Psalm

On any Monday   Psalm 126 (page 103)

(or)

Week 1	Psalm 49	*Week 3*	Psalm 104.26-end
Week 2	Psalm 65	*Week 4*	Psalm 50.1-15

Each psalm or group of psalms may end with

All   **Glory to the Father and to the Son**
and to the Holy Spirit;
as it was in the beginning is now,
and shall be for ever. Amen.

Short readings

Week One

The Lord called me before I was born, while I was in my mother's
womb he named me. He made my mouth like a sharp sword, in the
shadow of his hand he hid me; he made me a polished arrow, in his
quiver he hid me away. And he said to me, 'You are my servant,
Israel, in whom I will be glorified.' But I said, 'I have laboured in vain,
I have spent my strength for nothing and vanity; yet surely my cause
is with the Lord, and my reward with my God.'   *Isaiah 49.1b-4*

Week Two

Do not be wise in your own eyes; fear the Lord, and turn away from
evil. It will be a healing for your flesh and a refreshment for your
body. Honour the Lord with your substance and with the first fruits
of all your produce; then your barns will be filled with plenty, and
your vats will be bursting with wine. My child, do not despise the
Lord's discipline or be weary of his reproof, for the Lord reproves
the one he loves, as a father the son in whom he delights.

Proverbs 3.7-12

Jesus said, 'The kingdom of God is as if someone would scatter seed on the ground, and would sleep and rise night and day, and the seed would sprout and grow, he does not know how. The earth produces of itself, first the stalk, then the head, then the full grain in the head. But when the grain is ripe, at once he goes in with his sickle, because the harvest has come.'   *Mark 4.26-29*

Week Four

After a long time the master of those slaves came and settled accounts with them. Then the one who had received the five talents came forward, bringing five more talents, saying, 'Master, you handed over to me five talents; see, I have made five more talents.' His master said to him, 'Well done, good and trustworthy slave; you have been trustworthy in a few things, I will put you in charge of many things; enter into the joy of your master.'   *Matthew 25.19-21*

Or, on any Monday

Jesus said, 'Come to me, all you that are weary and are carrying heavy burdens, and I will give you rest.'   *Matthew 11.28*

Response

Silence, study, song, or words from Scripture, such as

Jesus said, I am the true vine.

All   **My Father is glorified by this, that you bear much fruit.**

John 15.1a,8

Prayers

Prayers may include these concerns:

¶ *The media and the arts*
¶ *Farming and fishing*
¶ *Commerce and industry*
¶ *Those whose work is unfulfilling, stressful or fraught with danger*
¶ *All who are unemployed*

The Collect of the day or the following prayer is said

Eternal light, shine into our hearts,
eternal goodness, deliver us from evil,
eternal power, be our support,
eternal wisdom, scatter the darkness of our ignorance,
eternal pity, have mercy upon us;
that with all our heart and mind and soul and strength
we may seek your face and be brought by your infinite mercy
     to your holy presence;
through Jesus Christ our Lord.

All **Amen.**   *Alcuin of York (804)*

The Lord's Prayer is said (inside back cover).

The Conclusion

May God bless the work of our hands.

All **Amen.**

¶ Prayer During the Day on Tuesday

Preparation

O God, make speed to save us.
All **O Lord, make haste to help us.**

To you, O Lord, I lift up my soul.
All **O my God, in you I trust.** *Psalm 25.1a*

Praise

A hymn, song, canticle, extempore praise or

I am giving you worship with all my life,
I am giving you obedience with all my power,
I am giving you praise with all my strength,
I am giving you honour with all my speech.

I am giving you love with all my heart,
I am giving you affection with all my sense,
I am giving you my being with all my mind,
I am giving you my soul, O most high and holy God.

Praise to the Father,
Praise to the Son,
Praise to the Spirit,
The Three in One. *adapted from Alexander Carmichael,*
Carmina Gadelica (1900)

The Word of God

Psalm

On any Tuesday Psalm 17.1-8 (page 90)

(or)

Week 1	Psalm 16	*Week 3*	Psalm 36
Week 2	Psalm 25	*Week 4*	Psalm 39

Each psalm or group of psalms may end with

All **Glory to the Father and to the Son
and to the Holy Spirit;
as it was in the beginning is now,
and shall be for ever. Amen.**

Short readings

Week One

If you will only obey the Lord your God, by diligently observing all
his commandments that I am commanding you today, the Lord your
God will set you high above all the nations of the earth; all these
blessings shall come upon you and overtake you, if you obey the
Lord your God: Blessed shall you be in the city, and blessed shall
you be in the field. Blessed shall be the fruit of your womb, the fruit
of your ground, and the fruit of your livestock, both the increase of
your cattle and the issue of your flock. Blessed shall be your basket
and your kneading-bowl. Blessed shall you be when you come in,
and blessed shall you be when you go out. *Deuteronomy 28.1-6*

They shall see the glory of the Lord, the majesty of our God. Strengthen the weak hands, and make firm the feeble knees. Say to those who are of a fearful heart, 'Be strong, do not fear! Here is your God. He will come with vengeance, with terrible recompense. He will come and save you.' Then the eyes of the blind shall be opened, and the ears of the deaf unstopped; then the lame shall leap like a deer, and the tongue of the speechless sing for joy. For waters shall break forth in the wilderness, and streams in the desert.

Isaiah 35.2c-6

Week Three

As Jesus walked along, he saw a man blind from birth. His disciples asked him, 'Rabbi, who sinned, this man or his parents, that he was born blind?' Jesus answered, 'Neither this man nor his parents sinned; he was born blind so that God's works might be revealed in him. We must work the works of him who sent me while it is day; night is coming when no one can work. As long as I am in the world, I am the light of the world.' *John 9.1-5*

Week Four

Then the angel showed me the river of the water of life, bright as crystal, flowing from the throne of God and of the Lamb through the middle of the street of the city. On either side of the river is the tree of life with its twelve kinds of fruit, producing its fruit each month; and the leaves of the tree are for the healing of the nations.

Revelation 22.1,2

Or, on any Tuesday

Great crowds came to Jesus, bringing with them the lame, the maimed, the blind, the mute, and many others. They put them at his feet, and he cured them. *Matthew 15.30*

Response ·

Silence, study, song, or words from Scripture, such as

Jesus said, I am the light of the world.

All **Whoever follows me will have the light of life.** *John 8.12*

Prayers

Prayers may include these concerns:

¶ *All who are sick in body, mind or spirit*

¶ *Those in the midst of famine or disaster*

¶ *Victims of abuse and violence, intolerance and prejudice*

¶ *Those who are bereaved*

¶ *All who work in the medical and healing professions*

The Collect of the day or the following prayer is said

Eternal God,
the light of the minds that know you,
the joy of the hearts that love you,
and the strength of the wills that serve you:
grant us so to know you
that we may truly love you,
so to love you that we may truly serve you,
whose service is perfect freedom;
through Jesus Christ our Lord.

All **Amen.**   *after Augustine of Hippo (430)*

The Lord's Prayer is said (inside back cover).

The Conclusion

May Christ our redeemer bring us healing and wholeness.

All **Amen.**

¶ *Prayer During the Day on Wednesday*

Preparation

O God, make speed to save us.
All **O Lord, make haste to help us.**

Make me to know your ways, O Lord,
All **and teach me your paths**. *Psalm 25.3*

Praise

A hymn, song, canticle, extempore praise or

You, Christ, are the King of glory,
the eternal Son of the Father.
When you took our flesh to set us free
you humbly chose the Virgin's womb.
You overcame the sting of death
and opened the kingdom of heaven to all believers.
You are seated at God's right hand in glory.

from Te Deum Laudamus

The Word of God

Psalm

On any Wednesday   Psalm 48 (pages 96–97)

(or)

Week 1	Psalm 2	*Week 3*	Psalm 45
Week 2	Psalm 44	*Week 4*	Psalm 72.1-8

Each psalm or group of psalms may end with

All **Glory to the Father and to the Son**
and to the Holy Spirit;
as it was in the beginning is now
and shall be for ever. Amen.

Short readings

Week One

The spirit of the Lord God is upon me, because the Lord has
anointed me; he has sent me to bring good news to the oppressed,
to bind up the broken-hearted, to proclaim liberty to the captives,
and release to the prisoners; to proclaim the year of the Lord's
favour, and the day of vengeance of our God; to comfort all who
mourn; to provide for those who mourn in Zion – to give them a
garland instead of ashes, the oil of gladness instead of mourning, the
mantle of praise instead of a faint spirit.   *Isaiah 61.1-3a*

Week Two

In days to come the mountain of the Lord's house shall be established as the highest of the mountains, and shall be raised up above the hills. Peoples shall stream to it, and many nations shall come and say: 'Come, let us go up to the mountain of the Lord, to the house of the God of Jacob; that he may teach us his ways and that we may walk in his paths.' For out of Zion shall go forth instruction, and the word of the Lord from Jerusalem. He shall judge between many peoples, and shall arbitrate between strong nations far away; they shall beat their swords into ploughshares, and their spears into pruning-hooks; nation shall not lift up sword against nation, neither shall they learn war any more; but they shall all sit under their own vines and under their own fig trees, and no one shall make them afraid.   *Micah 4.1-4a*

Week Three

Jesus went about all the cities and villages, teaching in their synagogues, and proclaiming the good news of the kingdom, and curing every disease and every sickness. When he saw the crowds, he had compassion for them, because they were harassed and helpless, like sheep without a shepherd. Then he said to his disciples, 'The harvest is plentiful, but the labourers are few; therefore ask the Lord of the harvest to send out labourers into his harvest.'
Matthew 9.35-end

Week Four

Pilate entered the headquarters again, summoned Jesus, and asked him, 'Are you the King of the Jews?' Jesus answered, 'My kingdom is not from this world. If my kingdom were from this world, my followers would be fighting to keep me from being handed over to the Jews. But as it is, my kingdom is not from here.' Pilate asked him, 'So you are a king?' Jesus answered, 'You say that I am a king. For this I was born, and for this I came into the world, to testify to the truth. Everyone who belongs to the truth listens to my voice.' Pilate asked him, 'What is truth?'   *John 18.33,36-38*

Or, on any Wednesday

The earth will be filled with the knowledge of the glory of the Lord, as the waters cover the sea.   *Habakkuk 2.14*

Response

Silence, study, song, or words from Scripture, such as

Jesus said, I am the way, and the truth, and the life.

All **No one comes to the Father except through me.**   *John 14.6*

Prayers

Prayers may include these concerns:

¶   *The social services*
¶   *All who work in the criminal justice system*
¶   *Victims and perpetrators of crime*
¶   *The work of aid agencies throughout the world*
¶   *Those living in poverty or under oppression*

The Collect of the day or the following prayer is said

O Lord our God,
grant us grace to desire you with our whole heart;
that so desiring, we may seek and find you;
and so finding, may love you;
and so loving, may hate those sins from which
    you have delivered us;
through Jesus Christ our Lord.

All **Amen.**   *Anselm (1109)*

The Lord's Prayer is said (inside back cover).

The Conclusion

May God grant to the world justice, truth and peace.

All **Amen.**

¶ Prayer During the Day on Thursday

Preparation

O God, make speed to save us.
All **O Lord, make haste to help us.**

Teach me to do what pleases you, for you are my God;
All **let your kindly spirit lead me on a level path.**   *Psalm 143.10*

Praise

A hymn, song, canticle, extempore praise or

Come, my Way, my Truth, my Life:
Such a Way, as gives us breath:
Such a Truth, as ends all strife:
And such a Life, as killeth death.

Come, my Light, my Feast, my Strength:
Such a Light, as shows a Feast:
Such a Feast, as mends in length:
Such a Strength, as makes his guest.

Come, my Joy, my Love, my Heart:
Such a Joy, as none can move:
Such a Love, as none can part:
Such a Heart, as joys in Love.   *George Herbert (1633)*

The Word of God

Psalm

On any Thursday   Psalm 133 (page 104)

(or)

Week 1	Psalm 81	*Week 3*	Psalm 101
Week 2	Psalm 90	*Week 4*	Psalm 107.1-16

Each psalm or group of psalms may end with

All   **Glory to the Father and to the Son
and to the Holy Spirit;
as it was in the beginning is now
and shall be for ever. Amen.**

Short readings

Week One

If there is among you anyone in need, a member of your community in any of your towns within the land that the Lord your God is giving you, do not be hard-hearted or tight-fisted towards your needy neighbour. You should rather open your hand, willingly lending enough to meet the need, whatever it may be. Give liberally and be ungrudging when you do so, for on this account the Lord your God will bless you in all your work and in all that you undertake. Since there will never cease to be some in need on the earth, I therefore command you, 'Open your hand to the poor and needy neighbour in your land.'   *Deuteronomy 15.7,8,10,11*

Do not fear, for I am with you; I will bring your offspring from the east, and from the west I will gather you; I will say to the north, 'Give them up', and to the south, 'Do not withhold; bring my sons from far away and my daughters from the end of the earth – everyone who is called by my name, whom I created for my glory, whom I formed and made.' *Isaiah 43.5-7*

Week Three

You are a chosen race, a royal priesthood, a holy nation, God's own people, in order that you may proclaim the mighty acts of him who called you out of darkness into his marvellous light. Once you were not a people, but now you are God's people; once you had not received mercy, but now you have received mercy. *I Peter 2.9,10*

Week Four

As you have sent me into the world, so I have sent them into the world. And for their sakes I sanctify myself, so that they also may be sanctified in truth. I ask not only on behalf of these, but also on behalf of those who will believe in me through their word, that they may all be one. As you, Father, are in me and I am in you, may they also be in us, so that the world may believe that you have sent me. The glory that you have given me I have given them, so that they may be one, as we are one, I in them and you in me, that they may become completely one, so that the world may know that you have sent me and have loved them even as you have loved me.

John 17.18-23

Or, on any Thursday

Just as the body is one and has many members, and all the members of the body, though many, are one body, so it is with Christ. For in the one Spirit we were all baptized into one body.

I Corinthians 12.12,13a

Response

Silence, study, song, or words from Scripture, such as

Jesus said, I am the gate for the sheep.

All **I came that they may have life, and have it abundantly.**

John 10.7,10b

Prayers

Prayers may include these concerns:

¶ *Local government, community leaders*
¶ *All who provide local services*
¶ *Those who work with young or elderly people*
¶ *Schools, colleges and universities*
¶ *Emergency and rescue organizations*

The Collect of the day or the following prayer is said

O gracious and holy Father,
give us wisdom to perceive you,
diligence to seek you,
patience to wait for you,
eyes to behold you,
a heart to meditate upon you,
and a life to proclaim you,
through the power of the Spirit
of Jesus Christ our Lord.

All **Amen.** *Benedict of Nursia (c.550)*

The Lord's Prayer is said (inside back cover).

The Conclusion

May God kindle in us the fire of love.
All **Amen.**

¶ *Prayer During the Day on Friday*

Preparation

O God, make speed to save us.
All **O Lord, make haste to help us.**

Make me a clean heart, O God,
All **and renew a right spirit within me.**   *Psalm 51.11*

Praise

A hymn, song, canticle, extempore praise or

Jesus, Saviour of the world,
    come to us in your mercy:
we look to you to save and help us.

By your cross and your life laid down,
    you set your people free:
we look to you to save and help us.

When they were ready to perish, you saved your disciples:
we look to you to come to our help.

In the greatness of your mercy, loose us from our chains,
forgive the sins of all your people.

Make yourself known as our Saviour and mighty deliverer;
save us and help us that we may praise you.

Come now and dwell with us, Lord Christ Jesus:
hear our prayer and be with us always.

And when you come in your glory:
make us to be one with you
    and to share the life of your kingdom.

The Word of God

Psalm

On any Friday   Psalm 23 (page 94)

(or)

Week 1   Psalm 112   *Week 3*   Psalm 123
Week 2   Psalm 120   *Week 4*   Psalm 124

Each psalm or group of psalms may end with

All   **Glory to the Father and to the Son
and to the Holy Spirit;
as it was in the beginning is now
and shall be for ever. Amen.**

Short readings

Week One

When I shut up the heavens so that there is no rain, or command
the locust to devour the land, or send pestilence among my people,
if my people who are called by my name humble themselves, pray,
seek my face, and turn from their wicked ways, then I will hear from
heaven, and will forgive their sin and heal their land.

2 Chronicles 7.13,14

Week Two

Thus says the high and lofty one who inhabits eternity, whose name is Holy: I dwell in the high and holy place, and also with those who are contrite and humble in spirit, to revive the spirit of the humble, and to revive the heart of the contrite. For I will not continually accuse, nor will I always be angry; for then the spirits would grow faint before me, even the souls that I have made. Because of their wicked covetousness I was angry; I struck them, I hid and was angry; but they kept turning back to their own ways. I have seen their ways, but I will heal them; I will lead them and repay them with comfort, creating for their mourners the fruit of the lips. Peace, peace, to the far and the near, says the Lord; and I will heal them.   *Isaiah 57.15-19*

Week Three

Now in Christ Jesus you who once were far off have been brought near by the blood of Christ. For he is our peace; in his flesh he has made both groups into one and has broken down the dividing wall, that is, the hostility between us. He has abolished the law with its commandments and ordinances, so that he might create in himself one new humanity in place of the two, thus making peace, and might reconcile both groups to God in one body through the cross, thus putting to death that hostility through it. So he came and proclaimed peace to you who were far off and peace to those who were near; for through him both of us have access in one Spirit to the Father.
Ephesians 2.13-18

Week Four

Jesus said to the disciples, 'The Son of Man must undergo great suffering, and be rejected by the elders, chief priests, and scribes, and be killed, and on the third day be raised.' Then he said to them all, 'If any want to become my followers, let them deny themselves and take up their cross daily and follow me. For those who want to save their life will lose it, and those who lose their life for my sake will save it. What does it profit them if they gain the whole world, but lose or forfeit themselves?'   *Luke 9.22-25*

Or, on any Friday

Jesus said, 'Love your enemies, do good to those who hate you, bless those who curse you, pray for those who abuse you.'   *Luke 6.27b,28*

Response

Silence, study, song, or words from Scripture, such as

Jesus said, I am the good shepherd.

All **The good shepherd lays down his life for the sheep.**

John 10.11

Prayers

Prayers may include these concerns:

¶ *The Queen, members of parliament and the armed forces*
¶ *Peace and justice in the world*
¶ *Those who work for reconciliation*
¶ *All whose lives are devastated by war and civil strife*
¶ *Prisoners, refugees and homeless people*

The Collect of the day or the following prayer is said

Lord Jesus Christ, we thank you
for all the benefits that you have won for us,
for all the pains and insults that you have borne for us.
Most merciful redeemer,
friend and brother,
may we know you more clearly,
love you more dearly,
and follow you more nearly,
day by day.

All **Amen.** *after Richard of Chichester (1253)*

The Lord's Prayer is said (inside back cover).

The Conclusion

May Christ our Saviour give us peace.
All **Amen.**

¶ Prayer During the Day on Saturday

Preparation

O God, make speed to save us.

All **O Lord, make haste to help us.**

Your love, O Lord, reaches to the heavens

All **and your faithfulness to the clouds.** *Psalm 36.5*

Praise

A hymn, song, canticle, extempore praise or

What shall I give you, Lord, in return for all your kindness?
Glory to you for your love.
Glory to you for your patience.
Glory to you for forgiving us all our sins.
Glory to you for coming to save our souls.
Glory to you for your incarnation in the virgin's womb.
Glory to you for your bonds.
Glory to you for receiving the cut of the lash.
Glory to you for accepting mockery.
Glory to you for your crucifixion.
Glory to you for your burial.
Glory to you for your resurrection.
Glory to you that you were preached to all.
Glory to you in whom they believed. *Ephrem the Syrian (373)*

The Word of God

On any Saturday   Psalm 63.1-8 (page 99)

(or)

| *Week 1* | Psalm 130 | *Week 3* | Psalm 138 |
| *Week 2* | Psalm 131 | *Week 4* | Psalm 139 |

Each psalm or group of psalms may end with

All   **Glory to the Father and to the Son**
and to the Holy Spirit;
as it was in the beginning is now
and shall be for ever. Amen.

Short readings

Week One

The wolf shall live with the lamb, the leopard shall lie down with the kid, the calf and the lion and the fatling together, and a little child shall lead them. The cow and the bear shall graze, their young shall lie down together; and the lion shall eat straw like the ox. The nursing child shall play over the hole of the asp, and the weaned child shall put its hand on the adder's den. They will not hurt or destroy on all my holy mountain; for the earth will be full of the knowledge of the Lord as the waters cover the sea.   *Isaiah 11.6-9*

Week Two

For this reason I bow my knees before the Father, from whom every family in heaven and earth takes its name. I pray that, according to the riches of his glory, he may grant that you may be strengthened in your inner being with power through his Spirit, and that Christ may dwell in your hearts through faith, as you are being rooted and grounded in love. I pray that you may have the power to comprehend, with all the saints, what is the breadth and length and height and depth, and to know the love of Christ that surpasses knowledge, so that you may be filled with all the fullness of God.

Ephesians 3.14-19

Week Three

When Jesus arrived, he found that Lazarus had already been in the tomb for four days. Now Bethany was near Jerusalem, some two miles away, and many of the Jews had come to Martha and Mary to console them about their brother. When Martha heard that Jesus was coming, she went and met him, while Mary stayed at home. Martha said to Jesus, 'Lord, if you had been here, my brother would not have died. But even now I know that God will give you whatever you ask of him.' Jesus said to her, 'Your brother will rise again.' Martha said to him, 'I know that he will rise again in the resurrection on the last day.' Jesus said to her, 'I am the resurrection and the life. Those who believe in me, even though they die, will live, and everyone who lives and believes in me will never die.'

John 11.17-26a

Week Four

When the Lamb had taken the scroll, the four living creatures and the twenty-four elders fell before the Lamb, each holding a harp and golden bowls full of incense, which are the prayers of the saints. They sing a new song: 'You are worthy to take the scroll and to open its seals, for you were slaughtered and by your blood you ransomed for God saints from every tribe and language and people and nation; you have made them to be a kingdom and priests serving our God, and they will reign on earth.' *Revelation 5.8-10*

Or, on any Saturday

We look not at what can be seen but at what cannot be seen; for what can be seen is temporary, but what cannot be seen is eternal.

2 Corinthians 4.18

Response

Silence, study, song, or words from Scripture, such as

Jesus said, I am the resurrection and the life.

All **Those who believe in me will never die.**

cf John 11.25,26

Prayers

Prayers may include these concerns:

¶ *Our homes, families, friends and all whom we love*
¶ *Those whose time is spent caring for others*
¶ *Those who are close to death*
¶ *Those who have lost hope*
¶ *The worship of the Church*

The Collect of the day or the following prayer is said

God be in my head, and in my understanding;
God be in my eyes, and in my looking;
God be in my mouth, and in my speaking;
God be in my heart, and in my thinking;
God be at mine end, and at my departing.

All **Amen.**

Sarum Primer

The Lord's Prayer is said (inside back cover).

The Conclusion

May Christ dwell in our hearts by faith.

All **Amen.**

¶ *Prayer During the Day*
Advent

From the First Sunday of Advent until Christmas Eve.

Preparation

O God, make speed to save us.

All **O Lord, make haste to help us.**

Your words have I hidden within my heart,

All **that I should not sin against you.**   *Psalm 119.11*

Praise

A hymn, song, canticle, extempore praise or

Saviour eternal,
life of the world unfailing,
light everlasting
and our true redemption.

Taking our humanity
in your loving freedom,
you rescued our lost earth
and filled the world with joy.

By your first advent justify us,
by your second, set us free:
that when the great light dawns
and you come as judge of all,
we may be robed in immortality
and ready, Lord, to follow
in your footsteps blest, wherever they may lead.

Salus Aeterna

The Word of God

Psalm

On any day   Psalm 80.1-8 (page 101)

(or)

Sunday	Psalm 82	*Thursday*	Psalm 70
Monday	Psalm 13	*Friday*	Psalm 75
Tuesday	Psalm 14	*Saturday*	Psalm 85
Wednesday	Psalm 54		

Each psalm or group of psalms may end with

All   **Glory to the Father and to the Son**
and to the Holy Spirit;
as it was in the beginning is now
and shall be for ever. Amen.

Short readings

Sunday

The Spirit and the bride say, 'Come.' And let everyone who hears say, 'Come.' And let everyone who is thirsty come. Let anyone who wishes take the water of life as a gift. The one who testifies to these things says, 'Surely I am coming soon.' Amen. Come, Lord Jesus! The grace of the Lord Jesus be with all the saints. Amen.

Revelation 22.17,20,21

Monday

A shoot shall come out from the stock of Jesse, and a branch shall grow out of his roots. The spirit of the Lord shall rest on him, the spirit of wisdom and understanding, the spirit of counsel and might, the spirit of knowledge and the fear of the Lord. His delight shall be in the fear of the Lord. He shall not judge by what his eyes see, or decide by what his ears hear; but with righteousness he shall judge the poor, and decide with equity for the meek of the earth; he shall strike the earth with the rod of his mouth, and with the breath of his lips he shall kill the wicked. *Isaiah 11.1-4*

Tuesday

The beginning of the good news of Jesus Christ, the Son of God. As it is written in the prophet Isaiah, 'See, I am sending my messenger ahead of you, who will prepare your way; the voice of one crying out in the wilderness: "Prepare the way of the Lord, make his paths straight." ' John the baptizer appeared in the wilderness, proclaiming a baptism of repentance for the forgiveness of sins. And people from the whole Judean countryside were going out to him, and were baptized by him in the river Jordan, confessing their sins. *Mark 1.1-5*

Wednesday

Jesus said to his disciples, 'Be dressed for action and have your lamps lit; be like those who are waiting for their master to return from the wedding banquet, so that they may open the door for him as soon as he comes and knocks. Blessed are those slaves whom the master finds alert when he comes; truly I tell you, he will fasten his belt and have them sit down to eat, and he will come and serve them.' *Luke 12.35-37*

Thursday

Jesus said to Peter, James, John and Andrew, 'It is like a man going on a journey, when he leaves home and puts his slaves in charge, each with his work, and commands the doorkeeper to be on the watch. Therefore, keep awake – for you do not know when the master of the house will come, in the evening, or at midnight, or at cockcrow, or at dawn, or else he may find you asleep when he comes suddenly. And what I say to you I say to all: Keep awake.' *Mark 13.34-end*

You know what time it is, how it is now the moment for you to wake from sleep. For salvation is nearer to us now than when we became believers; the night is far gone, the day is near. Let us then lay aside the works of darkness and put on the armour of light; let us live honourably as in the day, not in revelling and drunkenness, not in debauchery and licentiousness, not in quarrelling and jealousy. Instead, put on the Lord Jesus Christ, and make no provision for the flesh, to gratify its desires.   *Romans 13.11-end*

Saturday

The angel said to Mary, 'The Holy Spirit will come upon you, and the power of the Most High will overshadow you; therefore the child to be born will be holy; he will be called Son of God.' Then Mary said, 'Here am I, the servant of the Lord; let it be with me according to your word.' Then the angel departed from her.

Luke 1.35,38

Or, on any day in Advent

Comfort, O comfort my people, says your God.   *Isaiah 40.1*

Response

Silence, study, song, or words from Scripture, such as

Blessed are those who hunger and thirst for righteousness,

All **for they will be filled.**   *Matthew 5.6*

Prayers

Prayers may include these concerns:

¶ *The Church, that she may be ready for the coming of Christ*
¶ *The leaders of the Church*
¶ *The nations, that they may be subject to the rule of God*
¶ *Those who are working for justice in the world*
¶ *The broken, that they may find God's healing*

Keep us, O Lord,
while we tarry on this earth,
in a serious seeking after you,
and in an affectionate walking with you,
every day of our lives;
that when you come,
we may be found not hiding our talent,
nor serving the flesh,
nor yet asleep with our lamp unfurnished,
but waiting and longing for our Lord,
our glorious God for ever.

All **Amen.** *Richard Baxter (1691)*

The Lord's Prayer is said (inside back cover).

The Conclusion

May the Lord make us ready for his coming in glory.

All **Amen.**

¶ *Prayer During the Day*
Christmas Season

From Christmas Day until 5 January.

Preparation

O God, make speed to save us.

All **O Lord, make haste to help us.**

I will give thanks to you, Lord, with my whole heart;

All **I will tell of all your marvellous works.** *Psalm 9.1*

Praise

A hymn, song, canticle, extempore praise or

Glory to God in the highest,
and peace to his people on earth.
Lord God, heavenly King,
almighty God and Father,
we worship you, we give you thanks,
we praise you for your glory. *from Gloria in Excelsis*

The Word of God

Psalm

On Christmas Day and any day Psalm 8 (page 89)

(or)

Sunday	Psalm 113	*Thursday*	Psalm 127
Monday	Psalm 87	*Friday*	Psalm 128
Tuesday	Psalm 97	*Saturday*	Psalm 150
Wednesday	Psalm 110		

All **Glory to the Father and to the Son**
and to the Holy Spirit;
as it was in the beginning is now
and shall be for ever. Amen.

Short readings

Sunday

The Word became flesh and lived among us, and we have seen
his glory, the glory as of a father's only son, full of grace and truth.
From his fullness we have all received, grace upon grace. The law
indeed was given through Moses; grace and truth came through
Jesus Christ. No one has ever seen God. It is God the only Son,
who is close to the Father's heart, who has made him known.

John 1.14,16-18

Monday

The people who walked in darkness have seen a great light; those
who lived in a land of deep darkness – on them light has shined.
For a child has been born for us, a son given to us; authority rests
upon his shoulders; and he is named Wonderful Counsellor, Mighty
God, Everlasting Father, Prince of Peace. His authority shall grow
continually, and there shall be endless peace for the throne of David
and his kingdom. He will establish and uphold it with justice and
with righteousness from this time onwards and for evermore.
The zeal of the Lord of hosts will do this. *Isaiah 9.2,6,7*

Tuesday

An angel of the Lord appeared to Joseph in a dream and said,
'Joseph, son of David, do not be afraid to take Mary as your wife,
for the child conceived in her is from the Holy Spirit. She will bear
a son, and you are to name him Jesus, for he will save his people
from their sins.' All this took place to fulfil what had been spoken
by the Lord through the prophet: 'Look, the virgin shall conceive
and bear a son, and they shall name him Emmanuel', which means,
'God is with us.' *Matthew 1.20b-23*

Wednesday

The shepherds went with haste and found Mary and Joseph, and the child lying in the manger. When they saw this, they made known what had been told them about this child; and all who heard it were amazed at what the shepherds told them. But Mary treasured all these words and pondered them in her heart. The shepherds returned, glorifying and praising God for all they had heard and seen, as it had been told them.   *Luke 2.16-20*

Thursday

When the fullness of time had come, God sent his Son, born of a woman, born under the law, in order to redeem those who were under the law, so that we might receive adoption as children. And because you are children, God has sent the Spirit of his Son into our hearts, crying, 'Abba! Father!' So you are no longer a slave but a child, and if a child then also an heir, through God.   *Galatians 4.4-7*

Friday

The grace of God has appeared, bringing salvation to all, training us to renounce impiety and worldly passions, and in the present age to live lives that are self-controlled, upright, and godly, while we wait for the blessed hope and the manifestation of the glory of our great God and Saviour, Jesus Christ. He it is who gave himself for us that he might redeem us from all iniquity and purify for himself a people of his own who are zealous for good deeds.   *Titus 2.11-14*

Saturday

Long ago God spoke to our ancestors in many and various ways by the prophets, but in these last days he has spoken to us by a Son, whom he appointed heir of all things, through whom he also created the worlds. He is the reflection of God's glory and the exact imprint of God's very being, and he sustains all things by his powerful word.

Hebrews 1.1-3a

Or, on any day of Christmas

In him was life, and the life was the light of all people. The light shines in the darkness, and the darkness did not overcome it.   *John 1.4,5*

Response

Silence, study, song, or words from Scripture, such as

Blessed are the pure in heart,

All **for they will see God.** *Matthew 5.8*

Prayers

Prayers may include these concerns

¶ *The Church, especially in places of conflict*
¶ *The Holy Land, for peace with justice, and reconciliation*
¶ *Refugees and asylum seekers*
¶ *Homeless people*
¶ *Families with young children*

The Collect of the day or the following prayer is said

Almighty and everlasting God,
who stooped to raise fallen humanity
through the child-bearing of blessed Mary;
grant that we, who have seen your glory
　　revealed in our human nature
and your love made perfect in our weakness,
may daily be renewed in your image
and conformed to the pattern of your Son
Jesus Christ our Lord.

All **Amen.** *Collect of the Blessed Virgin Mary*

The Lord's Prayer is said (inside back cover).

The Conclusion

May the grace of Christ our Saviour be with us all.

All **Amen.**

Preparation

O God, make speed to save us.

All **O Lord, make haste to help us.**

With you, O God, is the well of life

All **and in your light shall we see light.**   *cf Psalm 36.9*

Praise

A hymn, song, canticle, extempore praise or

Christ Jesus was revealed in the flesh
and vindicated in the spirit.

He was seen by angels
and proclaimed among the nations.

Believed in throughout the world,
he was taken up in glory.

This will be made manifest at the proper time
by the blessed and only Sovereign,

Who alone has immortality,
and dwells in unapproachable light.

To the King of kings and Lord of lords
be honour and eternal dominion. Amen.

1 Timothy 3.16; 6.15,16

The Word of God

Psalm

On the Feast of the Epiphany and any day   Psalm 72.10-15 (page 100)

(or)

Sunday	Psalm 67	*Thursday*	Psalm 132.10-19
Monday	Psalm 99	*Friday*	Psalm 138
Tuesday	Psalm 100	*Saturday*	Psalm 149
Wednesday	Psalm 122		

Each psalm or group of psalms may end with

All **Glory to the Father and to the Son**
and to the Holy Spirit;
as it was in the beginning is now
and shall be for ever. Amen.

Short readings

Sunday

From the rising of the sun to its setting my name is great among
the nations, and in every place incense is offered to my name,
and a pure offering; for my name is great among the nations,
says the Lord of hosts.   *Malachi 1.11*

Monday

The steward said to the bridegroom, 'Everyone serves the good
wine first, and then the inferior wine after the guests have become
drunk. But you have kept the good wine until now.' Jesus did this,
the first of his signs, in Cana of Galilee, and revealed his glory;
and his disciples believed in him.   *John 2.10,11*

Tuesday

Arise, shine; for your light has come, and the glory of the Lord has risen upon you. For darkness shall cover the earth, and thick darkness the peoples; but the Lord will arise upon you, and his glory will appear over you. Nations shall come to your light, and kings to the brightness of your dawn.   *Isaiah 60.1-3*

Wednesday

We do not proclaim ourselves; we proclaim Jesus Christ as Lord and ourselves as your slaves for Jesus' sake. For it is the God who said, 'Let light shine out of darkness,' who has shone in our hearts to give the light of the knowledge of the glory of God in the face of Jesus Christ.   *2 Corinthians 4.5,6*

Thursday

You did not receive a spirit of slavery to fall back into fear, but you have received a spirit of adoption. When we cry, 'Abba! Father!' it is that very Spirit bearing witness with our spirit that we are children of God, and if children, then heirs, heirs of God and joint heirs with Christ – if, in fact, we suffer with him so that we may also be glorified with him.   *Romans 8.15-17*

Friday

With all wisdom and insight the Father has made known to us the mystery of his will, according to his good pleasure that he set forth in Christ, as a plan for the fullness of time, to gather up all things in him, things in heaven and things on earth.   *Ephesians 1.8b-10*

Saturday

In the midst of the lampstands I saw one like the Son of Man, clothed with a long robe and with a golden sash across his chest. His head and his hair were white as white wool, white as snow; his eyes were like a flame of fire, his feet were like burnished bronze, refined as in a furnace, and his voice was like the sound of many waters. In his right hand he held seven stars, and from his mouth came a sharp, two-edged sword, and his face was like the sun shining with full force.   *Revelation 1.13-16*

Or, on any day in Epiphany

Jesus said, 'I am the light of the world. Whoever follows me will never walk in darkness but will have the light of life.'   *John 8.12*

Response

Silence, study, song, or words from Scripture, such as

Blessed are the meek,

All **for they will inherit the earth.** *Matthew 5.5*

Prayers

Prayers may include these concerns:

¶ *The unity of the Church*
¶ *The peace of the world*
¶ *The healing of the sick*
¶ *The revelation of Christ to those from whom his glory is hidden*
¶ *All who travel*

The Collect of the day or the following prayer is said

O good Jesus,
Word of the Father and
    brightness of his glory,
whom angels desire to behold:
teach me to do your will
that, guided by your Spirit,
I may come to that blessed city of
    everlasting day,
where all are one in heart and mind,
where there is safety and eternal peace,
happiness and delight,
where you live with the Father and the Holy Spirit,
world without end.

All **Amen.** *after Gregory the Great (604)*

The Lord's Prayer is said (inside back cover).

The Conclusion

May the light of Christ our Lord shine in all our hearts.

All **Amen.**

¶ Prayer During the Day
Lent

From Ash Wednesday until the day before the Fifth Sunday of Lent.

Preparation

O God, make speed to save us.

All **O Lord, make haste to help us.**

Hear my prayer, O Lord, and give ear to my cry;

All **hold not your peace at my tears.**   *Psalm 39.13*

Praise

A hymn, song, canticle, extempore praise or

Jesus, like a mother you gather your people to you;
you are gentle with us as a mother with her children.

Despair turns to hope through your sweet goodness;
through your gentleness we find comfort in fear.

Your warmth gives life to the dead,
your touch makes sinners righteous.

Lord Jesus, in your mercy heal us;
in your love and tenderness remake us.

In your compassion bring grace and forgiveness,
for the beauty of heaven may your love prepare us.

Anselm (1109)

The Word of God

Psalm

On Ash Wednesday and any day Psalm 51.1-10 (page 98)

(or)

Sunday	Psalm 51.11-end	*Thursday*	Psalm 12
Monday	Psalm 3	*Friday*	Psalm 32
Tuesday	Psalm 6	*Saturday*	Psalm 61
Wednesday	Psalm 11		

Each psalm or group of psalms may end with

All **Glory to the Father and to the Son**
and to the Holy Spirit;
as it was in the beginning is now
and shall be for ever. Amen.

Short readings

Sunday

Do you not know that all of us who have been baptized into Christ Jesus were baptized into his death? Therefore we have been buried with him by baptism into death, so that, just as Christ was raised from the dead by the glory of the Father, so we too might walk in newness of life. For if we have been united with him in a death like his, we will certainly be united with him in a resurrection like his.

Romans 6.3-5

Monday

Yet even now, says the Lord, return to me with all your heart, with fasting, with weeping, and with mourning; rend your hearts and not your clothing. Return to the Lord, your God, for he is gracious and merciful, slow to anger, and abounding in steadfast love, and relents from punishing. Who knows whether he will not turn and relent, and leave a blessing behind him, a grain-offering and a drink-offering for the Lord, your God? *Joel 2.12-14*

Tuesday

Do you not know that in a race the runners all compete, but only one receives the prize? Run in such a way that you may win it. Athletes exercise self-control in all things; they do it to receive a perishable garland, but we an imperishable one. So I do not run aimlessly, nor do I box as though beating the air; but I punish my body and enslave it, so that after proclaiming to others I myself should not be disqualified.   *I Corinthians 9.24-end*

Wednesday

I find it to be a law that when I want to do what is good, evil lies close at hand. For I delight in the law of God in my inmost self, but I see in my members another law at war with the law of my mind, making me captive to the law of sin that dwells in my members. Wretched man that I am! Who will rescue me from this body of death? Thanks be to God through Jesus Christ our Lord!

Romans 7.21-25a

Thursday

Is not this the fast that I choose: to loose the bonds of injustice, to undo the thongs of the yoke, to let the oppressed go free, and to break every yoke? Is it not to share your bread with the hungry, and bring the homeless poor into your house; when you see the naked, to cover them, and not to hide yourself from your own kin? Then your light shall break forth like the dawn, and your healing shall spring up quickly; your vindicator shall go before you, the glory of the Lord shall be your rearguard. Then you shall call, and the Lord will answer; you shall cry for help, and he will say, Here I am.

Isaiah 58.6-9a

Friday

Jesus said to the disciples, 'Beware of practising your piety before others in order to be seen by them; for then you have no reward from your Father in heaven. So whenever you give alms, do not sound a trumpet before you, as the hypocrites do in the synagogues and in the streets, so that they may be praised by others. Truly I tell you, they have received their reward. But when you give alms, do not let your left hand know what your right hand is doing, so that your alms may be done in secret; and your Father who sees in secret will reward you.'   *Matthew 6.1-4*

Jesus entered a certain village, where a woman named Martha welcomed him into her home. She had a sister named Mary, who sat at the Lord's feet and listened to what he was saying. But Martha was distracted by her many tasks; so she came to Jesus and asked, 'Lord, do you not care that my sister has left me to do all the work by myself? Tell her then to help me.' But the Lord answered her, 'Martha, Martha, you are worried and distracted by many things; there is need of only one thing. Mary has chosen the better part, which will not be taken away from her.' *Luke 10.38-end*

Or, on any day in Lent

Jesus said, 'There will be more joy in heaven over one sinner who repents than over ninety-nine righteous people who need no repentance.' *Luke 15.7*

Response

Silence, study, song, or words from Scripture, such as

Blessed are the merciful,

All **for they will receive mercy.** *Matthew 5.7*

Prayers

Prayers may include these concerns

¶ *Those preparing for baptism and confirmation*
¶ *Those serving through leadership*
¶ *Those looking for forgiveness*
¶ *Those misled by the false gods of this present age*
¶ *All who are hungry*

The Collect of the day or the following prayer is said

Teach us, good Lord, to serve you as you deserve;
to give and not to count the cost;
to fight and not to heed the wounds;
to toil and not to seek for rest;
to labour and not to seek for any reward,
save that of knowing that we do your will.

All **Amen.** *Ignatius of Loyola (1556)*

The Lord's Prayer is said (inside back cover).

The Conclusion

May God bless us and show us compassion and mercy.

All **Amen.**

¶ *Prayer During the Day*
Passiontide

The last two weeks of Lent, from the Fifth Sunday of Lent until Easter Eve.

Preparation

O God, make speed to save us.

All **O Lord, make haste to help us.**

My trust is in you, O Lord.

All **I have said, 'You are my God.'**   *Psalm 31.14*

Praise

A hymn, song, canticle, extempore praise or

We adore you, O Christ, and we bless you,
because by your holy cross you have redeemed the world.

Holy God,
holy and strong,
holy and immortal,
have mercy upon us.

We glory in your cross, O Lord,
and praise and glorify your holy resurrection:
for by virtue of the cross
joy has come to the whole world.   *from the Liturgy of Good Friday*

The Word of God

Psalm

On Good Friday and any day   Psalm 22.1-11 (page 93)

(or)

Sunday	Psalm 27.1-8	*Thursday*	Psalm 23
Monday	Psalm 43	*Friday*	Psalm 69.1-13
Tuesday	Psalm 142	*Saturday*	Psalm 130
Wednesday	Psalm 143		

Each psalm or group of psalms may end with

All **Glory to the Father and to the Son
and to the Holy Spirit;
as it was in the beginning is now
and shall be for ever. Amen.**

Short readings

Sunday

It was fitting that God, for whom and through whom all things exist,
in bringing many children to glory, should make the pioneer of their
salvation perfect through sufferings. For the one who sanctifies and
those who are sanctified all have one Father. For this reason Jesus is
not ashamed to call them brothers and sisters, saying, 'I will
proclaim your name to my brothers and sisters, in the midst of the
congregation I will praise you.'   *Hebrews 2.10-12*

Monday

Jesus began to teach his disciples that the Son of Man must undergo great suffering, and be rejected by the elders, the chief priests, and the scribes, and be killed, and after three days rise again. He said all this quite openly. And Peter took him aside and began to rebuke him. But turning and looking at his disciples, he rebuked Peter and said, 'Get behind me, Satan! For you are setting your mind not on divine things but on human things.' He called the crowd with his disciples, and said to them, 'If any want to become my followers, let them deny themselves and take up their cross and follow me. For those who want to save their life will lose it, and those who lose their life for my sake, and for the sake of the gospel, will save it.'

Mark 8.31-35

Tuesday

Surely he has borne our infirmities and carried our diseases; yet we accounted him stricken, struck down by God, and afflicted. But he was wounded for our transgressions, crushed for our iniquities; upon him was the punishment that made us whole, and by his bruises we are healed. All we like sheep have gone astray; we have all turned to our own way, and the Lord has laid on him the iniquity of us all.

Isaiah 53.4-6

Wednesday

The message about the cross is foolishness to those who are perishing, but to us who are being saved it is the power of God. For Jews demand signs and Greeks desire wisdom, but we proclaim Christ crucified, a stumbling-block to Jews and foolishness to Gentiles, but to those who are the called, both Jews and Greeks, Christ the power of God and the wisdom of God. For God's foolishness is wiser than human wisdom, and God's weakness is stronger than human strength.

1 Corinthians 1.18,22-25

Thursday

Christ himself bore our sins in his body on the cross, so that, free from sins, we might live for righteousness; by his wounds you have been healed. For you were going astray like sheep, but now you have returned to the shepherd and guardian of your souls.

1 Peter 2.24,25

While we were still weak, at the right time Christ died for the ungodly. Indeed, rarely will anyone die for a righteous person – though perhaps for a good person someone might actually dare to die. But God proves his love for us in that while we still were sinners Christ died for us.   *Romans 5.6-8*

Saturday

Jesus answered Andrew and Philip, 'The hour has come for the Son of Man to be glorified. Very truly, I tell you, unless a grain of wheat falls into the earth and dies, it remains just a single grain; but if it dies, it bears much fruit. Those who love their life lose it, and those who hate their life in this world will keep it for eternal life. Whoever serves me must follow me, and where I am, there will my servant be also. Whoever serves me, the Father will honour.'   *John 12.23-26*

Or, on any day in Passiontide

I have been crucified with Christ; and it is no longer I who live, but it is Christ who lives in me.   *Galatians 2.19b,20a*

Response

Silence, study, song, or words from Scripture, such as

Blessed are those who are persecuted for righteousness' sake,

All **for theirs is the kingdom of heaven.**   *Matthew 5.10*

Prayers

Prayers may include these concerns

¶ *The persecuted Church*
¶ *The oppressed peoples of the world*
¶ *All who are lonely*
¶ *All who are near to death*
¶ *All who are facing loss*

The Collect of the day or the following prayer is said

Soul of Christ, sanctify me,
body of Christ, save me,
blood of Christ, inebriate me,
water from the side of Christ, wash me.
Passion of Christ, strengthen me.
O good Jesus, hear me:
hide me within your wounds
and never let me be separated from you.
From the wicked enemy defend me,
in the hour of my death, call me
and bid me come to you,
so that with your saints I may praise you
for ever and ever.

All **Amen.**   *Anima Christi (14th century)*

The Lord's Prayer is said (inside back cover).

The Conclusion

May Christ our Saviour give us peace.

All **Amen.**

¶ *Prayer During the Day*
Easter Season

From Easter Day until the day before Ascension Day.

Preparation

O God, make speed to save us.
All **O Lord, make haste to help us.**

If I climb up to heaven, you are there;
All **if I make the grave my bed, you are there also.**   *Psalm 139.7*

Praise

A hymn, song, canticle, extempore praise or

Yesterday I was crucified with Christ;
today I am glorified with him.
Yesterday I was dead with Christ;
today I am sharing in his resurrection.
Yesterday I was buried with him;
today I am waking with him from the sleep of death.
Gregory of Nazianzus (389)

The Word of God

Psalm

On Easter Day and any day   Psalm 118.14-24 (page 102)

(or)

Sunday	Psalm 114	*Thursday*	Psalm 111
Monday	Psalm 30	*Friday*	Psalm 145.1-8
Tuesday	Psalm 66.1-11	*Saturday*	Psalm 146
Wednesday	Psalm 106.1-12		

All **Glory to the Father and to the Son**
and to the Holy Spirit;
as it was in the beginning is now
and shall be for ever. Amen.

Short readings

Sunday

Blessed be the God and Father of our Lord Jesus Christ! By his great mercy he has given us a new birth into a living hope through the resurrection of Jesus Christ from the dead, and into an inheritance that is imperishable, undefiled, and unfading, kept in heaven for you, who are being protected by the power of God through faith for a salvation ready to be revealed in the last time.   *I Peter 1.3-5*

Monday

Sing aloud, O daughter Zion; shout, O Israel! Rejoice and exult with all your heart, O daughter Jerusalem! The Lord has taken away the judgements against you, he has turned away your enemies. The king of Israel, the Lord, is in your midst; you shall fear disaster no more. On that day it shall be said to Jerusalem: Do not fear, O Zion; do not let your hands grow weak. The Lord, your God, is in your midst, a warrior who gives victory; he will rejoice over you with gladness, he will renew you in his love; he will exult over you with loud singing as on a day of festival. I will remove disaster from you, so that you will not bear reproach for it.   *Zephaniah 3.14-18*

Tuesday

So it is with the resurrection of the dead. What is sown is perishable, what is raised is imperishable. It is sown in dishonour, it is raised in glory. It is sown in weakness, it is raised in power. It is sown a physical body, it is raised a spiritual body. The first man was from the earth, a man of dust; the second man is from heaven. As was the man of dust, so are those who are of the dust; and, as is the man of heaven, so are those who are of heaven. Just as we have borne the image of the man of dust, we will also bear the image of the man of heaven.   *I Corinthians 15.42-44a,47-49*

Wednesday

If you have been raised with Christ, seek the things that are above, where Christ is, seated at the right hand of God. Set your minds on things that are above, not on things that are on earth, for you have died, and your life is hidden with Christ in God. When Christ who is your life is revealed, then you also will be revealed with him in glory.

Colossians 3.1-4

Thursday

As the two disciples came near the village to which they were going, Jesus walked ahead as if he were going on. But they urged him strongly, saying, 'Stay with us, because it is almost evening and the day is now nearly over.' So he went in to stay with them. When he was at the table with them, he took bread, blessed and broke it, and gave it to them. Then their eyes were opened, and they recognized him; and he vanished from their sight. They said to each other, 'Were not our hearts burning within us while he was talking to us on the road, while he was opening the scriptures to us?'

Luke 24.28-32

Friday

Job said, 'O that my words were written down! O that they were inscribed in a book! O that with an iron pen and with lead they were engraved on a rock for ever! For I know that my Redeemer lives, and that at the last he will stand upon the earth; and after my skin has been thus destroyed, then in my flesh I shall see God, whom I shall see on my side, and my eyes shall behold, and not another.'

Job 19.23-27a

Saturday

I turned to see whose voice it was that spoke to me, and on turning I saw seven golden lampstands, and in the midst of the lampstands I saw one like the Son of Man, clothed with a long robe and with a golden sash across his chest. When I saw him, I fell at his feet as though dead. But he placed his right hand on me, saying, 'Do not be afraid; I am the first and the last, and the living one. I was dead, and see, I am alive for ever and ever; and I have the keys of Death and of Hades.'   *Revelation 1.12,13,17,18*

Or, on any day in Easter

Jesus said, 'This is the will of him who sent me, that I should lose nothing of all that he has given me, but raise it up on the last day.'

John 6.39

Response

Silence, study, song, or words from Scripture, such as

Blessed are the peacemakers,

All **for they will be called children of God.**   *Matthew 5.9*

Prayers

Prayers may include these concerns:

¶ *The people of God, that they may proclaim the risen Lord*
¶ *God's creation, that the peoples of the earth may meet their responsibility to care*
¶ *Those in despair and darkness, that they may find the hope and light of Christ*
¶ *Those in fear of death, that they may find faith through the resurrection*
¶ *Prisoners and captives*

The Collect of the day or the following prayer is said

Christ yesterday and today,
the beginning and the end,
Alpha and Omega,
all time belongs to you,
and all ages;
to you be glory and power
through every age and for ever.

All **Amen.**   *from the Easter Vigil*

The Lord's Prayer is said (inside back cover).

The Conclusion

May the risen Christ give us his peace.

All **Alleluia. Amen.**

¶ Prayer During the Day from Ascension Day until the Day of Pentecost

These last days of the Easter season are days of prayer and preparation for the outpouring of the Holy Spirit.

Preparation

O God, make speed to save us.

All **O Lord, make haste to help us.**

Gladden the soul of your servant,

All **for to you, O Lord, I lift up my soul.**　　　　　　*Psalm 86.4*

Praise

A hymn, song, canticle, extempore praise or

Blessed are you, the God of our ancestors,
worthy to be praised and exalted for ever.

Blessed is your holy and glorious name,
worthy to be praised and exalted for ever.

Blessed are you, in your holy and glorious temple,
worthy to be praised and exalted for ever.

Blessed are you who look into the depths,
worthy to be praised and exalted for ever.

Blessed are you, enthroned on the cherubim,
worthy to be praised and exalted for ever.

Blessed are you on the throne of your kingdom,
worthy to be praised and exalted for ever.

Blessed are you in the heights of heaven,
worthy to be praised and exalted for ever.

The Song of the Three 29-34

The Word of God

On Ascension Day and on any day Psalm 47 (page 96)

(or)

Sunday	Psalm 104.26-32	*Thursday*	Psalm 84
Monday	Psalm 21.1-7	*Friday*	Psalm 93
Tuesday	Psalm 29	*Saturday*	Psalm 98
Wednesday	Psalm 46		

Each psalm or group of psalms may end with

All **Glory to the Father and to the Son**
and to the Holy Spirit;
as it was in the beginning is now
and shall be for ever. Amen.

Short readings

Ascension Day or on any day after Ascension
Christ did not enter a sanctuary made by human hands, a mere copy
of the true one, but he entered into heaven itself, now to appear in
the presence of God on our behalf.   *Hebrews 9.24*

Friday after Ascension
As it is, we do not yet see everything in subjection to human beings,
but we do see Jesus, who for a little while was made lower than the
angels, now crowned with glory and honour because of the suffering
of death, so that by the grace of God he might taste death for
everyone. It was fitting that God, for whom and through whom
all things exist, in bringing many children to glory, should make
the pioneer of their salvation perfect through sufferings.
                                              Hebrews 2.8b-10

Saturday after Ascension

I am convinced that neither death, nor life, nor angels, nor rulers, nor things present, nor things to come, nor powers, nor height, nor depth, nor anything else in all creation, will be able to separate us from the love of God in Christ Jesus our Lord.   *Romans 8.38,39*

Sunday after Ascension

On the last day of the festival, the great day, while Jesus was standing there, he cried out, 'Let anyone who is thirsty come to me, and let the one who believes in me drink. As the scripture has said, "Out of the believer's heart shall flow rivers of living water." ' Now he said this about the Spirit, which believers in him were to receive.

John 7.37-39a

Monday

Have you not known? Have you not heard? The Lord is the everlasting God, the Creator of the ends of the earth. He does not faint or grow weary; his understanding is unsearchable. He gives power to the faint, and strengthens the powerless. Even youths will faint and be weary, and the young will fall exhausted; but those who wait for the Lord shall renew their strength, they shall mount up with wings like eagles, they shall run and not be weary, they shall walk and not faint.   *Isaiah 40.28-end*

Tuesday

Now there are varieties of gifts, but the same Spirit; and there are varieties of services, but the same Lord; and there are varieties of activities, but it is the same God who activates all of them in everyone. To each is given the manifestation of the Spirit for the common good.   *I Corinthians 12.4-7*

Wednesday

I will pour out my spirit on all flesh; your sons and your daughters shall prophesy, your old men shall dream dreams, and your young men shall see visions. Even on the male and female slaves, in those days, I will pour out my spirit.   *Joel 2.28,29*

Thursday

Jesus said, 'Ask, and it will be given to you; search, and you will find; knock, and the door will be opened for you. For everyone who asks receives, and everyone who searches finds, and for everyone who knocks, the door will be opened. Is there anyone among you who, if your child asks for a fish, will give a snake instead of a fish? Or if the child asks for an egg, will give a scorpion? If you then, who are evil, know how to give good gifts to your children, how much more will the heavenly Father give the Holy Spirit to those who ask him!'

Luke 11.9-13

Friday

In Christ every one of God's promises is a 'Yes'. For this reason it is through him that we say the 'Amen', to the glory of God. But it is God who establishes us with you in Christ and has anointed us, by putting his seal on us and giving us his Spirit in our hearts as a first instalment.   *2 Corinthians 1.20-22*

Saturday

The Lord is the Spirit, and where the Spirit of the Lord is, there is freedom. And all of us, with unveiled faces, seeing the glory of the Lord as though reflected in a mirror, are being transformed into the same image from one degree of glory to another; for this comes from the Lord, the Spirit.   *2 Corinthians 3.17,18*

The Day of Pentecost

Jesus said, 'Peace be with you. As the Father has sent me, so I send you.' When he had said this, he breathed on them and said to them, 'Receive the Holy Spirit.'   *John 20.21,22*

Response

Silence, study, song, or words from Scripture, such as

Blessed are those who mourn,

All **for they will be comforted.**   *Matthew 5.4*

Prayers

Prayers may include these concerns:

¶ *God's royal priesthood, that it may be empowered by the Spirit*
¶ *Those who wait on God, that they may find renewal*
¶ *All people, that they may acknowledge the kingdom of the ascended Christ*
¶ *The earth, for productivity and for fruitful harvests*
¶ *All who are struggling with broken relationships*

The Collect of the day or the following prayer is said

O King enthroned on high,
Comforter and Spirit of truth,
you that are in all places and fill all things,
the treasury of blessings and the giver of life,
come and dwell with us,
cleanse us from every stain
and save our souls, O gracious one.

All **Amen.**   *an Orthodox prayer*

The Lord's Prayer is said (inside back cover).

The Conclusion

May the grace of the Holy Spirit enlighten our hearts and minds.

All **Alleluia. Amen.**

¶ *Prayer During the Day from All Saints' Day until the day before the First Sunday of Advent*

This period is observed as a time of celebration and reflection on the reign of Christ in earth and in heaven.

Preparation

O God, make speed to save us.

All **O Lord, make haste to help us.**

You have been my helper

All **and under the shadow of your wings will I rejoice.**   *Psalm 63.8*

Praise

A hymn, song, canticle, extempore praise or

For the gift of his Spirit:
blessed be Christ.

For the catholic Church:
blessed be Christ.

For the means of grace:
blessed be Christ.

For the hope of glory:
blessed be Christ.

For the triumphs of his gospel:
blessed be Christ.

For the lives of his saints:
blessed be Christ.

In joy and in sorrow:
blessed be Christ.

In life and in death:
blessed be Christ.

Now and to the end of the ages:
blessed be Christ.   *from A Litany of the Resurrection*

The Word of God

Psalm

On All Saints' Day and on any day Psalm 24.1-6 (page 95)

(or)

Sunday	Psalm 2	*Thursday*	Psalm 121
Monday	Psalm 15	*Friday*	Psalm 125
Tuesday	Psalm 42.1-7	*Saturday*	Psalm 133
Wednesday	Psalm 96		

Each psalm or group of psalms may end with

All **Glory to the Father and to the Son**
and to the Holy Spirit;
as it was in the beginning is now
and shall be for ever. Amen.

Short readings

Sunday

Whenever the living creatures give glory and honour and thanks to the one who is seated on the throne, who lives for ever and ever, the twenty-four elders fall before the one who is seated on the throne and worship the one who lives for ever and ever; they cast their crowns before the throne, singing, 'You are worthy, our Lord and God, to receive glory and honour and power, for you created all things, and by your will they existed and were created.'

Revelation 4.9-end

Monday

Rejoice in the Lord always; again I will say, Rejoice. Let your gentleness be known to everyone. The Lord is near. Do not worry about anything, but in everything by prayer and supplication with thanksgiving let your requests be made known to God. And the peace of God, which surpasses all understanding, will guard your hearts and your minds in Christ Jesus. *Philippians 4.4-7*

Tuesday

You have come to Mount Zion and to the city of the living God, the heavenly Jerusalem, and to innumerable angels in festal gathering, and to the assembly of the firstborn who are enrolled in heaven, and to God the judge of all, and to the spirits of the righteous made perfect, and to Jesus, the mediator of a new covenant, and to the sprinkled blood that speaks a better word than the blood of Abel.

Hebrews 12.22-24

Wednesday

Then the sign of the Son of Man will appear in heaven, and then all the tribes of the earth will mourn, and they will see 'the Son of Man coming on the clouds of heaven' with power and great glory. And he will send out his angels with a loud trumpet call, and they will gather his elect from the four winds, from one end of heaven to the other.

Matthew 24.30,31

Thursday

The gifts he gave were that some would be apostles, some prophets, some evangelists, some pastors and teachers, to equip the saints for the work of ministry, for building up the body of Christ, until all of us come to the unity of the faith and of the knowledge of the Son of God, to maturity, to the measure of the full stature of Christ.

Ephesians 4.11-13

Friday

Since we are surrounded by so great a cloud of witnesses, let us also lay aside every weight and the sin that clings so closely, and let us run with perseverance the race that is set before us, looking to Jesus the pioneer and perfecter of our faith, who for the sake of the joy that was set before him endured the cross, disregarding its shame, and has taken his seat at the right hand of the throne of God.

Hebrews 12.1,2

Saturday

Many of those who sleep in the dust of the earth shall awake, some to everlasting life, and some to shame and everlasting contempt. Those who are wise shall shine like the brightness of the sky, and those who lead many to righteousness, like the stars for ever and ever.

Daniel 12.2,3

Or, on any day from All Saints to Advent

Our citizenship is in heaven, and it is from there that we are expecting a Saviour, the Lord Jesus Christ.   *Philippians 3.20*

Response

Silence, study, song, or words from Scripture, such as

Blessed are the poor in spirit,

All **for theirs is the kingdom of heaven.** *Matthew 5.3*

Prayers

Prayers may include these concerns

¶ *The saints on earth, that they may live as citizens of heaven*
¶ *All people, that they may hear and believe the word of God*
¶ *All who fear the winter months*
¶ *All sovereigns and political leaders, that they may imitate the righteous rule of Christ*
¶ *All who grieve or wait with the dying*

The Collect of the day or the following prayer is said

Bring us, O Lord God, at our last awakening
into the house and gate of heaven,
to enter that gate and dwell in that house,
where there shall be no darkness nor dazzling,
    but one equal light;
no noise nor silence, but one equal music;
no fears nor hopes, but one equal possession;
no ends or beginnings, but one equal eternity;
in the habitations of your glory and dominion,
world without end.

All **Amen.** *Eric Milner-White (1963)*
after John Donne (1631)

The Lord's Prayer is said (inside back cover).

The Conclusion

May God give us grace to follow his saints in glory.

All **Amen.**

Night Prayer

An Order for Night Prayer (Compline)

¶ *Introduction*

The ancient office of Compline derives its name from a Latin word meaning 'completion' *(completorium)*. It is above all a service of quietness and reflection before rest at the end of the day. It is most effective when the ending is indeed an ending, without additions, conversation or noise. If there is an address, or business to be done, it should come first. If the service is in church, those present depart in silence; if at home, they go quietly to bed.

Night Prayer (Compline)

Preparation

The minister **asks a blessing** on the life of all God's holy people.

Authorized Prayers of Penitence may be used.

A **hymn** may be sung.

The Word of God

This includes
- ¶ a **psalm or psalms**
- ¶ a **short reading from Holy Scripture**
- ¶ a **responsory**, committing oneself into the hands of God
- ¶ the **Gospel Canticle**: *Nunc dimittis*

Prayers

Intercessions and thanksgivings may be offered.

The Collect is said.

The Lord's Prayer may be said.

The Conclusion

The service concludes with
- ¶ **a calling on God for protection** through the coming night
- ¶ a simple **blessing**

¶ Notes

1   Gospel Reading

On suitable occasions, particularly Saturday night and before other festivals, the Gospel for the following day may be read before Night Prayer or in place of the set reading.

2   Thanksgiving

Reflection on the past day may lead into thanksgiving in addition to penitence.

3   Penitence

When the confession is used, it may be replaced by another act of penitence. However, all that precedes 'O God, make speed to save us' may be omitted; this is particularly appropriate if Holy Communion has been celebrated in the evening.

4   Scripture Reading

Other passages of Scripture may be read in place of those printed in the Order.

5   Alleluia

The Alleluias included in the Easter form of the Responsory are for use from Easter Day until the Day of Pentecost, not at other times. The Alleluia following the opening versicles and responses is always used, except in Lent.

6   Conclusion

The response in square brackets [ ] is normally used only if Holy Communion is to be celebrated the following morning.

An Order for Night Prayer (Compline)

Preparation

The Lord almighty grant us a quiet night and a perfect end.

All **Amen.**

Our help is in the name of the Lord

All **who made heaven and earth.**

A period of silence for reflection on the past day may follow.

The following or other suitable words of penitence may be used

All **Most merciful God,**
we confess to you,
before the whole company of heaven and one another,
that we have sinned in thought, word and deed
and in what we have failed to do.
Forgive us our sins,
heal us by your Spirit
and raise us to new life in Christ. Amen.

O God, make speed to save us.

All **O Lord, make haste to help us.**

All **Glory to the Father and to the Son**
and to the Holy Spirit;
as it was in the beginning is now
and shall be for ever. Amen.
Alleluia.

Before the ending of the day,
Creator of the world, we pray
That you, with steadfast love, would keep
Your watch around us while we sleep.

From evil dreams defend our sight,
From fears and terrors of the night;
Tread underfoot our deadly foe
That we no sinful thought may know.

O Father, that we ask be done
Through Jesus Christ, your only Son;
And Holy Spirit, by whose breath
Our souls are raised to life from death.

The Word of God

Psalmody

One or more of the following psalms may be used.

Psalm 4

1   Answer me when I call, O God of my righteousness; ♦
     you set me at liberty when I was in trouble;
          have mercy on me and hear my prayer.

2   How long will you nobles dishonour my glory; ♦
     how long will you love vain things and seek after falsehood?

3   But know that the Lord has shown me his marvellous kindness; ♦
     when I call upon the Lord, he will hear me.

4   Stand in awe, and sin not; ♦
     commune with your own heart upon your bed, and be still.

5   Offer the sacrifices of righteousness ♦
     and put your trust in the Lord.

6   There are many that say, 'Who will show us any good?' ♦
     Lord, lift up the light of your countenance upon us.

7   You have put gladness in my heart, ♦
       more than when their corn and wine and oil increase.

8   In peace I will lie down and sleep, ♦
       for it is you Lord, only, who make me dwell in safety.

Psalm 91

1   Whoever dwells in the shelter of the Most High ♦
       and abides under the shadow of the Almighty,

2   Shall say to the Lord, 'My refuge and my stronghold, ♦
       my God, in whom I put my trust.'

3   For he shall deliver you from the snare of the fowler ♦
       and from the deadly pestilence.

4   He shall cover you with his wings
           and you shall be safe under his feathers; ♦
       his faithfulness shall be your shield and buckler.

5   You shall not be afraid of any terror by night, ♦
       nor of the arrow that flies by day;

6   Of the pestilence that stalks in darkness, ♦
       nor of the sickness that destroys at noonday.

7   Though a thousand fall at your side
           and ten thousand at your right hand, ♦
       yet it shall not come near you.

8   Your eyes have only to behold ♦
       to see the reward of the wicked.

9   Because you have made the Lord your refuge ♦
       and the Most High your stronghold,

10   There shall no evil happen to you, ♦
       neither shall any plague come near your tent.

11   For he shall give his angels charge over you, ♦
       to keep you in all your ways.

12   They shall bear you in their hands, ♦
       lest you dash your foot against a stone.

13 You shall tread upon the lion and adder; ♦
    the young lion and the serpent you shall trample underfoot.

14 Because they have set their love upon me,
        therefore will I deliver them; ♦
    I will lift them up, because they know my name.

15 They will call upon me and I will answer them; ♦
    I am with them in trouble,
        I will deliver them and bring them to honour.

16 With long life will I satisfy them ♦
    and show them my salvation.

Psalm 134

1 Come, bless the Lord, all you servants of the Lord, ♦
   you that by night stand in the house of the Lord.

2 Lift up your hands towards the sanctuary ♦
   and bless the Lord.

3 The Lord who made heaven and earth ♦
   give you blessing out of Zion.

At the end of the psalmody, the following is said or sung

All **Glory to the Father and to the Son
and to the Holy Spirit;
as it was in the beginning is now
and shall be for ever. Amen.**

Scripture Reading

One of the following short lessons or another suitable passage is read

You, O Lord, are in the midst of us and we are called by your name;
leave us not, O Lord our God. *Jeremiah 14.9*

(or)

Be sober, be vigilant, because your adversary the devil is prowling
round like a roaring lion, seeking for someone to devour. Resist him,
strong in the faith. *1 Peter 5.8, 9*

(or)

The servants of the Lamb shall see the face of God, whose name will
be on their foreheads. There will be no more night: they will not
need the light of a lamp or the light of the sun, for God will be their
light, and they will reign for ever and ever. *Revelation 22.4, 5*

The following responsory may be said

Into your hands, O Lord, I commend my spirit.
All **Into your hands, O Lord, I commend my spirit.**
For you have redeemed me, Lord God of truth.
All **I commend my spirit.**
Glory to the Father and to the Son
and to the Holy Spirit.
All **Into your hands, O Lord, I commend my spirit.**

Or, in Easter

Into your hands, O Lord, I commend my spirit.
Alleluia, alleluia.
All **Into your hands, O Lord, I commend my spirit.
Alleluia, alleluia.**
For you have redeemed me, Lord God of truth.
All **Alleluia, alleluia.**
Glory to the Father and to the Son
and to the Holy Spirit.
All **Into your hands, O Lord, I commend my spirit.
Alleluia, alleluia.**

Keep me as the apple of your eye.
All **Hide me under the shadow of your wings.**

The Nunc dimittis (The Song of Simeon) is said or sung

All **Save us, O Lord, while waking,**
and guard us while sleeping,
that awake we may watch with Christ
and asleep may rest in peace.

1 Now, Lord, you let your servant go in peace: ◆
your word has been fulfilled.

2 My own eyes have seen the salvation ◆
which you have prepared in the sight of every people;

3 A light to reveal you to the nations ◆
and the glory of your people Israel.   *Luke 2.29-32*

All **Glory to the Father and to the Son**
and to the Holy Spirit;
as it was in the beginning is now
and shall be for ever. Amen.

All **Save us, O Lord, while waking,**
and guard us while sleeping,
that awake we may watch with Christ
and asleep may rest in peace.

Prayers

Intercessions and thanksgivings may be offered here.

The Collect

Silence may be kept.

Visit this place, O Lord, we pray,
and drive far from it the snares of the enemy;
may your holy angels dwell with us and guard us in peace,
and may your blessing be always upon us;
through Jesus Christ our Lord.

All **Amen.**

The Lord's Prayer may be said (inside back cover).

The Conclusion

In peace we will lie down and sleep;
All **for you alone, Lord, make us dwell in safety.**

Abide with us, Lord Jesus,
All **for the night is at hand and the day is now past.**

As the night watch looks for the morning,
All **so do we look for you, O Christ.**

[Come with the dawning of the day
All **and make yourself known in the breaking of the bread.**]

The Lord bless us and watch over us;
the Lord make his face shine upon us and be gracious to us;
the Lord look kindly on us and give us peace.
All **Amen.**

Psalms

Introduction

How to say or sing the Psalms

Psalms are essentially songs and are transformed if sung
(or spoken aloud), even when you are praying alone.

When two or more gather to worship, psalms may be said or sung
in different ways (and some psalms, or parts of psalms, lend
themselves to one method rather than another):

♦ by a single voice (everyone is encouraged to join in saying
  'Glory to the Father…' – see below – at the end);

♦ by everyone together;

♦ with the verses alternated between one half of the group
  and the other;

♦ with the verses alternated between the leader and the others;

♦ responsorially (see the note under 'refrains' below).

When saying a psalm aloud, the word 'blessed' is usually
pronounced as two syllables: 'bless - ed'. Where spelled 'blest',
the word is pronounced as one syllable.

A diamond ♦ marks the mid-point in each psalm verse,
at which point some people follow the custom of taking a pause.
Most verses of the psalms fall naturally into two halves and pausing
in the middle emphasizes this. People also find that it helps them
to concentrate on the meaning of what is being read.

A traditional Christian ending to each psalm or group of psalms is:

All   **Glory to the Father and to the Son
and to the Holy Spirit;
as it was in the beginning is now
and shall be for ever. Amen.**

Refrains

Each of the psalms has an optional refrain (sometimes called an antiphon).

The refrain can be used at the beginning and end of a psalm, by everybody, regardless of how the rest of the psalm is recited. (The refrain is used after the 'Glory to the Father…' and not immediately before it.)

The psalm can be recited 'responsorially'. One person reads or sings the psalm and the others join in with the response at beginning and end, and wherever there is a symbol [R].

Some psalms (such as Psalm 8) have integral refrains within the poetry. These are indicated by text in *italics*. If the psalm is being recited responsorially, these verses are recited by everyone, at the point at which they occur.

Psalm prayers

Each psalm is also provided with an optional short prayer, which develops a theme from the text. When it is used, it is best to omit the 'Glory to the Father…' and to keep a period of silence for individual reflection at the end of the psalm (after the refrain, when this is included), before the prayer itself is said.

These refrains and psalm prayers are merely suggestions: you can use the refrains only, or just the prayers – or neither.

Praying the Psalms

Within the Psalms all states of human experience and emotion are expressed to God, through good times and bad. If you do not identify with the situation addressed in the one that you are reciting, then take the opportunity to pray for someone who is in that situation instead. You may wish to pause after the psalm to pray about concerns that are raised within it.

1   *O Lord our governor,* ♦
    how glorious is your name in all the world!

2   Your majesty above the heavens is praised ♦
    out of the mouths of babes at the breast.

3   You have founded a stronghold against your foes, ♦
    that you might still the enemy and the avenger.

4   When I consider your heavens, the work of your fingers, ♦
    the moon and the stars that you have ordained,

5   What is man, that you should be mindful of him; ♦
    the son of man, that you should seek him out?

6   You have made him little lower than the angels ♦
    and crown him with glory and honour.

7   You have given him dominion over the works of your hands ♦
    and put all things under his feet,

8   All sheep and oxen, ♦
    even the wild beasts of the field,

9   The birds of the air, the fish of the sea ♦
    and whatsoever moves in the paths of the sea.

10 *O Lord our governor,* ♦
    how glorious is your name in all the world!

> *We bless you, master of the heavens,*
> *for the wonderful order which enfolds this world;*
> *grant that your whole creation*
> *may find fulfilment in the Son of Man,*
> *Jesus Christ our Saviour.*

Refrain: *Deliver me, O Lord, by your hand.*

1   Hear my just cause, O Lord; consider my complaint; ♦
     listen to my prayer, which comes not from lying lips.

2   Let my vindication come forth from your presence; ♦
     let your eyes behold what is right.

3   Weigh my heart, examine me by night, ♦
     refine me, and you will find no impurity in me. [R]

4   My mouth does not trespass for earthly rewards; ♦
     I have heeded the words of your lips.

5   My footsteps hold fast in the ways of your commandments; ♦
     my feet have not stumbled in your paths. [R]

6   I call upon you, O God, for you will answer me; ♦
     incline your ear to me, and listen to my words.

7   Show me your marvellous loving-kindness, ♦
     O Saviour of those who take refuge at your right hand
          from those who rise up against them.

8   Keep me as the apple of your eye; ♦
     hide me under the shadow of your wings.

     Refrain: *Deliver me, O Lord, by your hand.*

          Generous Lord,
          deliver us from all envious thoughts,
          and when we are tempted by the desire for wealth,
          let us see your face;
          for your abundance is enough to clothe our lack;
          through Jesus Christ our Lord.

Refrain: *The commandment of the Lord is pure
and gives light to the eyes.*

1   The heavens are telling the glory of God ♦
and the firmament proclaims his handiwork.

2   One day pours out its song to another ♦
and one night unfolds knowledge to another.

3   They have neither speech nor language ♦
and their voices are not heard,

4   Yet their sound has gone out into all lands ♦
and their words to the ends of the world.

5   In them has he set a tabernacle for the sun, ♦
that comes forth as a bridegroom out of his chamber
and rejoices as a champion to run his course.

6   It goes forth from the end of the heavens
and runs to the very end again, ♦
and there is nothing hidden from its heat. [R]

7   The law of the Lord is perfect, reviving the soul; ♦
the testimony of the Lord is sure
and gives wisdom to the simple.

8   The statutes of the Lord are right and rejoice the heart; ♦
the commandment of the Lord is pure
and gives light to the eyes.

9   The fear of the Lord is clean and endures for ever; ♦
the judgements of the Lord are true
and righteous altogether.

10   More to be desired are they than gold,
more than much fine gold, ♦
sweeter also than honey,
dripping from the honeycomb.

11   By them also is your servant taught ♦
and in keeping them there is great reward. [R]

12   Who can tell how often they offend? ♦
        O cleanse me from my secret faults!

13   Keep your servant also from presumptuous sins
           lest they get dominion over me; ♦
        so shall I be undefiled,
           and innocent of great offence.

14   Let the words of my mouth and the meditation of my heart
           be acceptable in your sight, ♦
        O Lord, my strength and my redeemer.

Refrain: *The commandment of the Lord is pure*
              and gives light to the eyes.

              Christ, the sun of righteousness,
              rise in our hearts this day,
              enfold us in the brightness of your love
              and bear us at the last to heaven's horizon;
              for your love's sake.

Refrain: *Be not far from me, O Lord.*

1   My God, my God, why have you forsaken me, ♦
    and are so far from my salvation,
        from the words of my distress?

2   O my God, I cry in the daytime,
        but you do not answer; ♦
    and by night also, but I find no rest.

3   Yet you are the Holy One, ♦
    enthroned upon the praises of Israel.

4   Our forebears trusted in you; ♦
    they trusted, and you delivered them.

5   They cried out to you and were delivered; ♦
    they put their trust in you and were not confounded. [R]

6   But as for me, I am a worm and no man, ♦
    scorned by all and despised by the people.

7   All who see me laugh me to scorn; ♦
    they curl their lips and wag their heads, saying,

8   'He trusted in the Lord; let him deliver him; ♦
    let him deliver him, if he delights in him.'

9   But it is you that took me out of the womb ♦
    and laid me safe upon my mother's breast.

10 On you was I cast ever since I was born; ♦
    you are my God even from my mother's womb.

11 Be not far from me, for trouble is near at hand ♦
    and there is none to help.

Refrain: *Be not far from me, O Lord.*

> *Restless with grief and fear,*
> *the abandoned turn to you:*
> *in every hour of trial,*
> *good Lord, deliver us,*
> *O God most holy, God most strong,*
> *whose wisdom is the cross of Christ.*

Refrain: *I will dwell in the house of the Lord for ever.*

1   The Lord is my shepherd; ♦
      therefore can I lack nothing.

2   He makes me lie down in green pastures ♦
      and leads me beside still waters. [R]

3   He shall refresh my soul ♦
      and guide me in the paths of righteousness for his name's sake.

4   Though I walk through the valley of the shadow of death,
          I will fear no evil; ♦
      for you are with me;
          your rod and your staff, they comfort me. [R]

5   You spread a table before me
          in the presence of those who trouble me; ♦
      you have anointed my head with oil
          and my cup shall be full.

6   Surely goodness and loving mercy shall follow me
          all the days of my life, ♦
      and I will dwell in the house of the Lord for ever.

Refrain: *I will dwell in the house of the Lord for ever.*

          O God, our sovereign and shepherd,
          who brought again your Son Jesus Christ
              from the valley of death,
          comfort us with your protecting presence
          and your angels of goodness and love,
          that we also may come home
          and dwell with him in your house for ever.

Refrain: *The Lord of hosts: he is the King of glory.*

1   The earth is the Lord's and all that fills it, ♦
    the compass of the world and all who dwell therein.

2   For he has founded it upon the seas ♦
    and set it firm upon the rivers of the deep. [R]

3   'Who shall ascend the hill of the Lord, ♦
    or who can rise up in his holy place?'

4   'Those who have clean hands and a pure heart, ♦
    who have not lifted up their soul to an idol,
        nor sworn an oath to a lie;

5   'They shall receive a blessing from the Lord, ♦
    a just reward from the God of their salvation.'

6   Such is the company of those who seek him, ♦
    of those who seek your face, O God of Jacob.

Refrain: *The Lord of hosts: he is the King of glory.*

> *O Lord of hosts,*
> *purify our hearts*
> *that the King of glory may come in,*
> *your Son, Jesus our redeemer.*

Refrain: *O sing praises to God, sing praises.*

1 Clap your hands together, all you peoples; ♦
   O sing to God with shouts of joy.

2 For the Lord Most High is to be feared; ♦
   he is the great King over all the earth.

3 He subdued the peoples under us ♦
   and the nations under our feet.

4 He has chosen our heritage for us, ♦
   the pride of Jacob, whom he loves. [R]

5 God has gone up with a merry noise, ♦
   the Lord with the sound of the trumpet.

6 O sing praises to God, sing praises; ♦
   sing praises to our King, sing praises.

7 For God is the King of all the earth; ♦
   sing praises with all your skill. [R]

8 God reigns over the nations; ♦
   God has taken his seat upon his holy throne.

9 The nobles of the peoples are gathered together ♦
   with the people of the God of Abraham.

10 For the powers of the earth belong to God ♦
    and he is very highly exalted.

   Refrain: *O sing praises to God, sing praises.*

          As Christ was raised by your glory, O Father,
          so may we be raised to new life
          and rejoice to be called your children,
          both now and for ever.

Psalm 48

Refrain: *We have waited on your loving-kindness, O God.*

1 Great is the Lord and highly to be praised, ♦
   in the city of our God.

2   His holy mountain is fair and lifted high, ♦
    the joy of all the earth.

3   On Mount Zion, the divine dwelling place, ♦
    stands the city of the great king.

4   In her palaces God has shown himself ♦
    to be a sure refuge. [R]

5   For behold, the kings of the earth assembled ♦
    and swept forward together.

6   They saw, and were dumbfounded; ♦
    dismayed, they fled in terror.

7   Trembling seized them there;
        they writhed like a woman in labour, ♦
    as when the east wind shatters the ships of Tarshish.

8   As we had heard, so have we seen
        in the city of the Lord of hosts, the city of our God: ♦
    God has established her for ever. [R]

9   We have waited on your loving-kindness, O God, ♦
    in the midst of your temple.

10 As with your name, O God,
        so your praise reaches to the ends of the earth; ♦
    your right hand is full of justice.

11 Let Mount Zion rejoice and the daughters of Judah be glad, ♦
    because of your judgements, O Lord.

12 Walk about Zion and go round about her;
        count all her towers; ♦
    consider well her bulwarks; pass through her citadels,

13 That you may tell those who come after
        that such is our God for ever and ever. ♦
    It is he that shall be our guide for evermore.

    Refrain: *We have waited on your loving-kindness, O God.*

                Father of lights,
                raise us with Christ to your eternal city,
                that, with kings and nations,
                we may wait in the midst of your temple
                and see your glory for ever and ever.

Refrain: *The sacrifice of God is a broken spirit.*

1   Have mercy on me, O God, in your great goodness; ♦
    according to the abundance of your compassion
        blot out my offences.

2   Wash me thoroughly from my wickedness ♦
    and cleanse me from my sin.

3   For I acknowledge my faults ♦
    and my sin is ever before me.

4   Against you only have I sinned ♦
    and done what is evil in your sight,

5   So that you are justified in your sentence ♦
    and righteous in your judgement. [R]

6   I have been wicked even from my birth, ♦
    a sinner when my mother conceived me.

7   Behold, you desire truth deep within me ♦
    and shall make me understand wisdom
        in the depths of my heart.

8   Purge me with hyssop and I shall be clean; ♦
    wash me and I shall be whiter than snow.

9   Make me hear of joy and gladness, ♦
    that the bones you have broken may rejoice.

10 Turn your face from my sins ♦
    and blot out all my misdeeds.

Refrain: *The sacrifice of God is a broken spirit.*

> *Take away, good Lord, the sin that corrupts us;*
> *give us the sorrow that heals*
> *and the joy that praises*
> *and restore by grace your own image within us,*
> *that we may take our place among your people;*
> *in Jesus Christ our Lord.*

Refrain: My soul is athirst for God, even for the living God.

1   O God, you are my God; eagerly I seek you; ♦
    my soul is athirst for you.

2   My flesh also faints for you, ♦
    as in a dry and thirsty land where there is no water.

3   So would I gaze upon you in your holy place, ♦
    that I might behold your power and your glory.

4   Your loving-kindness is better than life itself ♦
    and so my lips shall praise you.

5   I will bless you as long as I live ♦
    and lift up my hands in your name. [R]

6   My soul shall be satisfied, as with marrow and fatness, ♦
    and my mouth shall praise you with joyful lips,

7   When I remember you upon my bed ♦
    and meditate on you in the watches of the night.

8   For you have been my helper ♦
    and under the shadow of your wings will I rejoice.

Refrain: My soul is athirst for God, even for the living God.

To you we come, radiant Lord,
the goal of all our desiring,
beyond all earthly beauty;
gentle protector, strong deliverer,
in the night you are our confidence;
from first light be our joy;
through Jesus Christ our Lord.

Refrain: *The Lord is king; let the earth rejoice.*

10   The kings of Tarshish and of the isles shall pay tribute; ♦
      the kings of Sheba and Seba shall bring gifts.

11   All kings shall fall down before him; ♦
      all nations shall do him service. [R]

12   For he shall deliver the poor that cry out, ♦
      the needy and those who have no helper.

13   He shall have pity on the weak and poor; ♦
      he shall preserve the lives of the needy.

14   He shall redeem their lives from oppression and violence, ♦
      and dear shall their blood be in his sight. [R]

15   Long may he live;
          unto him may be given gold from Sheba; ♦
      may prayer be made for him continually
          and may they bless him all the day long.

Refrain: *The Lord is king; let the earth rejoice.*

May your kingdom come, O God,
with deliverance for the needy,
with peace for the righteous,
with overflowing blessing for all nations,
with glory, honour and praise
for Christ, the only Saviour.

1   Hear, O Shepherd of Israel, ♦
you that led Joseph like a flock;

2   Shine forth, you that are enthroned upon the cherubim, ♦
before Ephraim, Benjamin and Manasseh.

3   Stir up your mighty strength ♦
and come to our salvation.

4   *Turn us again, O God; ♦*
show the light of your countenance, and we shall be saved.

5   O Lord God of hosts, ♦
how long will you be angry at your people's prayer?

6   You feed them with the bread of tears; ♦
you give them abundance of tears to drink.

7   You have made us the derision of our neighbours, ♦
and our enemies laugh us to scorn.

8   *Turn us again, O God of hosts; ♦*
show the light of your countenance, and we shall be saved.

> *Faithful shepherd of your people,*
> *as we look for the light of your countenance,*
> *restore in us the image of your glory*
> *and graft us into the risen life of your Son,*
> *Jesus Christ our Lord.*

Refrain: I will give thanks to you,
                for you have become my salvation.

14   The Lord is my strength and my song, ♦
      and he has become my salvation.

15   Joyful shouts of salvation ♦
      sound from the tents of the righteous:

16   'The right hand of the Lord does mighty deeds;
         the right hand of the Lord raises up; ♦
      the right hand of the Lord does mighty deeds.'

17   I shall not die, but live ♦
      and declare the works of the Lord.

18   The Lord has punished me sorely, ♦
      but he has not given me over to death. [R]

19   Open to me the gates of righteousness, ♦
      that I may enter and give thanks to the Lord.

20   This is the gate of the Lord; ♦
      the righteous shall enter through it.

21   I will give thanks to you, for you have answered me ♦
      and have become my salvation.

22   The stone which the builders rejected ♦
      has become the chief cornerstone.

23   This is the Lord's doing, ♦
      and it is marvellous in our eyes.

24   This is the day that the Lord has made; ♦
      we will rejoice and be glad in it.

Refrain: I will give thanks to you,
                for you have become my salvation.

                Saving God,
                open the gates of righteousness,
                that your pilgrim people may enter
                and be built into a living temple
                on the cornerstone of our salvation,
                Jesus Christ our Lord.

Refrain: *The Lord has indeed done great things for us.*

1   When the Lord restored the fortunes of Zion, ♦
      then were we like those who dream.

2   Then was our mouth filled with laughter ♦
      and our tongue with songs of joy.

3   Then said they among the nations, ♦
      'The Lord has done great things for them.'

4   The Lord has indeed done great things for us, ♦
      and therefore we rejoiced. [R]

5   Restore again our fortunes, O Lord, ♦
      as the river beds of the desert.

6   Those who sow in tears ♦
      shall reap with songs of joy.

7   Those who go out weeping, bearing the seed, ♦
      will come back with shouts of joy,
            bearing their sheaves with them.

Refrain: *The Lord has indeed done great things for us.*

            Lord, as you send rain and flowers
            even to the wilderness,
            renew us by your Holy Spirit,
            help us to sow good seed in time of adversity
            and to live to rejoice in your good harvest of all creation;
            through Jesus Christ our Lord.

Refrain: *Mercy and truth are met together,*
                   righteousness and peace have kissed each other.

1   Behold how good and pleasant it is ♦
     to dwell together in unity.

2   It is like the precious oil upon the head, ♦
     running down upon the beard,

3   Even on Aaron's beard, ♦
     running down upon the collar of his clothing.

4   It is like the dew of Hermon ♦
     running down upon the hills of Zion.

5   For there the Lord has promised his blessing: ♦
     even life for evermore.

Refrain: *Mercy and truth are met together,*
                   righteousness and peace have kissed each other.

Grant to your people, good Lord,
the spirit of unity,
that they may dwell together in your love,
and so bear to the world
the ointment of your healing and the
    dew of your blessing;
through Jesus Christ our Lord.

Acknowledgements and Sources

Thanks are due to the following for permission to reproduce copyright material:

The Archbishops' Council of the Church of England: *Common Worship: Services and Prayers for the Church of England*, *Common Worship: President's Edition*, *Common Worship: Pastoral Services*, all of which are copyright © The Archbishops' Council of the Church of England.

Cambridge University Press: extracts (and adapted extracts) from *The Book of Common Prayer*, the rights in which are vested in the Crown, are reproduced by permission of the Crown's Patentee, Cambridge University Press.

The Division of Christian Education of the National Council of Churches in the USA: Scripture quotations from *The New Revised Standard Version of the Bible*, copyright © 1989 by the Division of Christian Education of the National Council of Churches in the USA. Used by permission. All rights reserved.

The English Language Liturgical Consultation: English translation of The Lord's Prayer, The Apostles' Creed, Gloria Patri, Benedictus, Magnificat, Nunc dimittis prepared by the English Language Liturgical Consultation, based on (or excerpted from) *Praying Together* © ELLC, 1988.

The European Province of the Society of St Francis: extracts adapted or excerpted from *Celebrating Common Prayer* © The Society of St Francis European Province 1992 and 1996. Used by permission.

¶ Authorization

The orders for Prayer During the Day and Night Prayer are taken from *Common Worship: Daily Prayer* (2005), which was published at the request of the House of Bishops of the General Synod of the Church of England.

These orders of service comply with the provisions of A Service of the Word, which is authorized pursuant to Canon B 2 of the Canons of the Church of England for use in public worship until further resolution of the Synod.

They include texts which have been authorized pursuant to Canon B 2 for use in public worship until further resolution of the General Synod, material commended by the House of Bishops and other material, the use of which falls within the discretion canonically allowed to the minister under Canon B 5.
(For details, see *Common Worship: Daily Prayer*, page 877.)

Copyright Information

The Archbishops' Council of the Church of England and the other copyright owners and administrators of texts included in *Common Worship: Daily Prayer*, material from which is included in this book, have given permission for the use of their material in local reproductions on a non-commercial basis which comply with the conditions for reproductions for local use set out in the Archbishops' Council's booklet, *A Brief Guide to Liturgical Copyright*. This is available from:

www.commonworship.com

A reproduction which meets the conditions stated in that booklet may be made without an application for copyright permission or payment of a fee, but the following copyright acknowledgement must be included:

> *Time to Pray*, material from which is included in this service, is copyright © The Archbishops' Council 2006.

Permission must be obtained in advance for any reproduction which does not comply with the conditions set out in *A Brief Guide to Liturgical Copyright*. Applications for permission should be addressed to:

The Copyright Administrator
The Archbishops' Council
Church House
Great Smith Street
London SW1P 3NZ
Telephone: 020 7898 1451
Fax: 020 7898 1449
Email: copyright@c-of-e.org.uk

The Lord's Prayer

As our Saviour taught us, so we pray

All   **Our Father in heaven,
hallowed be your name,
your kingdom come,
your will be done,
on earth as in heaven.
Give us today our daily bread.
Forgive us our sins
as we forgive those who sin against us.
Lead us not into temptation
but deliver us from evil.
For the kingdom, the power,
and the glory are yours
now and for ever.
Amen.**

(or)

Let us pray with confidence as our Saviour has taught us

All   **Our Father, who art in heaven,
hallowed be thy name;
thy kingdom come;
thy will be done;
on earth as it is in heaven.
Give us this day our daily bread.
And forgive us our trespasses,
as we forgive those who trespass against us.
And lead us not into temptation;
but deliver us from evil.
For thine is the kingdom,
the power and the glory,
for ever and ever.
Amen.**